P9-CFC-304

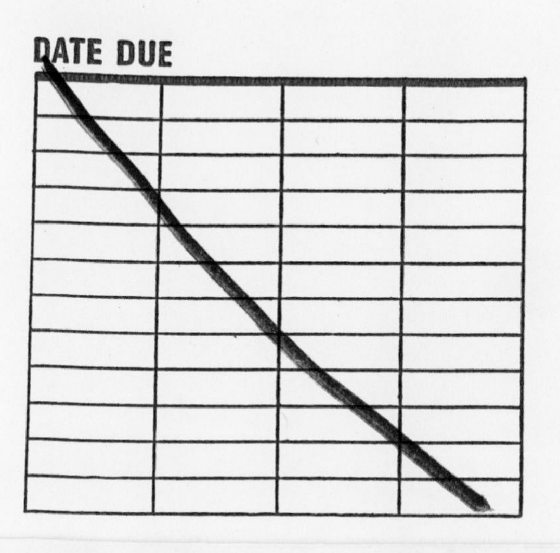
DATE DUE

Twayne's United States Authors Series

Sylvia E. Bowman, *Editor*

INDIANA UNIVERSITY

Norman Thomas

Photo courtesy The New York Times

NORMAN THOMAS

NORMAN THOMAS

By JAMES C. DURAM

Wichita State University

234

Twayne Publishers, Inc. :: New York

Library of Congress Cataloging in Publication Data
Duram, James C 1939-
Norman Thomas.

(Twayne's United States authors series, TUSAS 234)
Bibliography: p. 167.
1. Thomas, Norman Mattoon, 1884-1968.
HX84.T47D87 335'.0092'4 [B] 73-15831
ISBN 0-8057-0727-1

MANUFACTURED IN THE UNITED STATES OF AMERICA

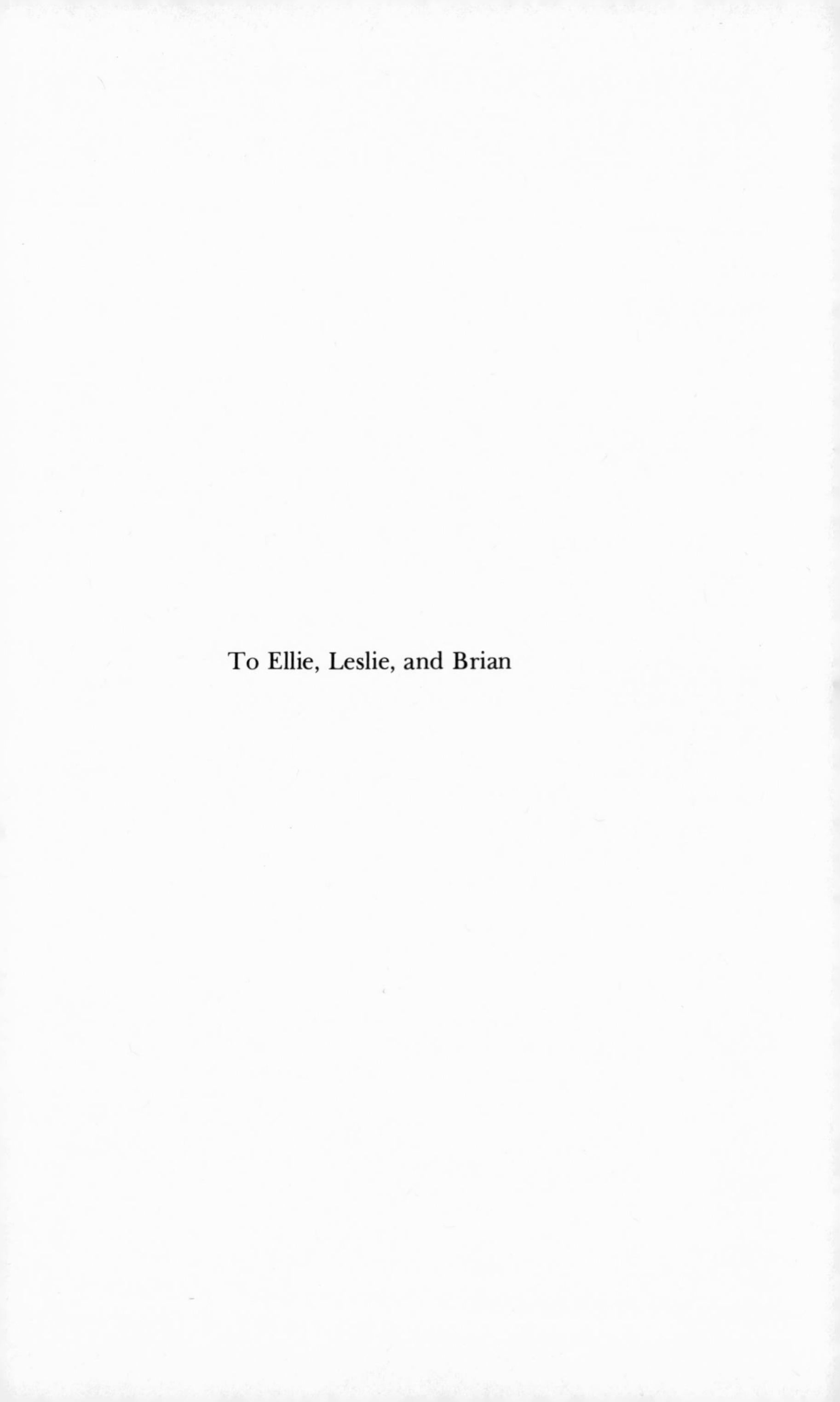

To Ellie, Leslie, and Brian

Preface

Norman Mattoon Thomas (1884-1968), who is often personified as the twentieth-century conscience of American reform, was an unrelenting critic-commentator about nearly all aspects of American society. Throughout his long life, he urged a generally uninterested American people to accept the principles of Democratic Socialism as a basic solution to the numerous problems confronting a rapidly changing society. While he is remembered much more at present for his remarkable ability as a persuasive speaker and for his participatory activism in defense of civil liberties and a variety of both popular and unpopular causes, Thomas was also a remarkably prolific writer of books, pamphlets, letters, and essays during his long and vigorous life. This volume is an examination of the significance of these writings.

A survey of the bibliography of works about Thomas indicates that, in marked contrast to the extensive writing about the political aspects of Norman Thomas' career, there is an absence of any serious attempt to examine the literary and intellectual currents which shaped his voluminous writing. Such a critical-analytical study of Thomas' writings seems worthwhile for two reasons: first, Thomas exerted a powerful influence on the American intellectual community during his lifetime and after; second, Norman Thomas represented the twentieth-century extension of an old and honorable tradition of American dissent and radicalism.

Norman Thomas' writing career began with his emergence as an advocate of pacifism and Socialism during World War I and ended only a few months prior to his death in 1968. Harry Fleischman, one of his two leading biographers, has characterized most of Thomas' literary efforts as "tracts for the times" rather than as great literature.[1] Nevertheless, his writing, spanning as it does his entire forty-year career as a political activist, furnishes an excellent means of examining the problems and opportunities encountered by the reformer-activist as a writer in twentieth-century America. Thomas regarded his writings as an important part of his attempt to persuade Americans that there were serious shortcomings in their society which had to be corrected. Thomas' books, essays, pamphlets, and letters read collectively like a vast, running compendium of his reactions to all of the major economic, political, and social issues which have been debated in the United States in this century. Norman Thomas' writing stands as the most voluminous and penetrating record of the literary expression of the American Socialist reform mind between World War I and the present. His writing provides a clear picture of the interaction of Romanticism and Realism which has marked so much of American Socialist reform thought.

The approach of this volume is simple in that the intent is to answer four basic questions about the writings of Norman Thomas. First, what were the major influences which shaped his writings? Second, what were the major themes and subjects in his writings? Third, what literary techniques and style did he use? Finally, what can be said about his significance as a writer? It is hoped that the pursuit of the answers to these questions will provide the reader with an increased appreciation of Norman Thomas as one of the leaders of a long and honorable tradition of American reform. Such an appreciation will, hopefully, lead the reader to enjoy firsthand the penetrating wisdom, wit, and sheer love of humanity which pervades the whole of Thomas' writings.

A final point is in order. Many of Norman Thomas' reform ideas were so closely related that some repetition in dealing with them could not be avoided. It is the author's hope that the reader will accept these instances in the same spirit of forbearance which Thomas would have shown were he alive today.

James C. Duram

Wichita State University
Wichita, Kansas

Acknowledgments

No book is ever really the product of a single individual. The author wishes to acknowledge the financial assistance of the National Endowment for the Humanities and the Wichita State University Faculty Research Fund in the preparation of this book. The kindness of Mr. Evan Thomas, who allowed me to examine the collection of his father's papers in the New York Public Library, and Mr. Maurice Goldbloom, who shared so generously of his memories of Norman Thomas, are deeply appreciated. Generous permission to quote from material in their publications was granted by: *The Christian Century, The Nation, The New Republic, The New York Times Magazine,* and *Saturday Review.* The permission granted by Brandt & Brandt, the literary agent for the Thomas Estate, to quote from a large number of Norman Thomas' books is also gratefully acknowledged. To my wife, Eleanor, goes a special thanks for her patience, advice, and technical assistance in the preparation of this manuscript. Finally, the author assumes responsibility for all of the errors in this work.

Contents

Chronology

1884 Norman Mattoon Thomas born in Marion, Ohio, November 20; the eldest of six children of the Reverend Welling Evan and Emma (Mattoon) Thomas.

1905 Graduates (valedictorian) with Bachelor of Arts degree from Princeton University. Becomes a social worker at the Spring Street Presbyterian Church and Settlement House, New York City.

1907 Goes on a trip around the world. Spends considerable time in Asia; becomes an opponent of colonialism.

1910 Marries Frances Violet Stewart, September 1; eventually has six children and fifteen grandchildren.

1910-1911 Serves as associate minister for the Brick Presbyterian Church, New York City, while attending Union Theological Seminary, a stronghold of Social Gospel doctrines.

1911 Ordained in the Presbyterian Church; receives Bachelor of Divinity degree. Becomes pastor of the East Harlem Presbyterian Church and director of the American Parish.

1912 Registers as a Progressive.

1917 Joins the Fellowship of Reconciliation and supports Morris Hillquit, the Socialist who campaigns as an anti-war candidate, for New York City mayor. Thomas and Roger N. Baldwin establish the National Civil Liberties Bureau (now the American Civil Liberties Union).

1918 Begins publishing *The New World* (soon renamed *The World Tomorrow);* serves as its editor until 1921. Resigns from his church responsibilities; becomes an active member of the Socialist party.

1921 Serves for one year as associate editor of *The Nation.*

1922 Thomas and Harry W. Laidler accept co-directorship of the League for Industrial Democracy.

1923 Edits the *New York Leader;* from 1924-35, contributes regularly to *The New Leader. The Conscientious Objector in America.*

1924 Runs for governor of New York as a Socialist-Progressive candidate.

1925 Runs for mayor of New York City as reform candidate.

1926 Arrested for addressing the striking wool workers in Passaic, New Jersey; grand jury refuses to indict him. Begins to assume the leadership of the Socialist party after the death of Eugene V. Debs.

1928 Runs for President on the Socialist ticket in what proves to be the first of six consecutive unsuccessful attempts.

1931 Leaves the ministry. *America's Way Out: A Program for Democracy.*

1932 Plays leading role in organizing the Southern Tenant Farmers' Union (now the Agricultural Workers' Union). *As I See It.* Thomas and Paul Blanshard publish *What's the Matter with New York: A National Problem.*

1934 *The Choice Before Us: Mankind at the Crossroads* and *Human Exploitation in the United States.*

1935 Supports the "Militants" in their intraparty struggle with the "Old Guard."

1936 *After the New Deal, What?*

1937 Takes a trip to Spain and the Soviet Union. Becomes even more disillusioned about Communism. Becomes a leading member of the Keep America Out of War Committee.

1938 *Socialism on the Defensive.*

1939 Thomas and Bertram D. Wolfe publish *Keep America Out of War: A Program.*

1941 Adopts policy of "critical support" toward United States' war effort. *We Have a Future.*

1942 Establishes The Post War World Council.

1947 His wife dies unexpectedly. *Appeal to the Nations.*

1949 Favors the reconstitution of the Socialist party as an educational and research body, not as a vote-seeking political party.

1950 Refuses to accept renomination to the Socialist party governing committees but remains the party's unofficial spokesman.

1951 *A Socialist's Faith.*

1954 *The Test of Freedom;* criticizes those who would destroy civil liberties in pursuit of internal security.

1959 *The Prerequisites for Peace.*

1960 One of the founders of the National Committee for a Sane Nuclear Policy. Starts contributing to the *New*

	America. Becomes actively involved in anti-Vietnam War activities by lecturing on numerous campuses.
1961	*Great Dissenters.*
1963	*Socialism Re-examined.*
1967	Suffers stroke; retires from public life.
1968	December 19, dies at the age of eighty-four and is memorialized as the conscience of America.
1969	His final book, *The Choices,* posthumously published.

CHAPTER *1*

The Shaping of the Reform Mind

NORMAN Thomas once requested that his biographers refrain from depicting him as a sentimental or heroic figure.[1] Despite his wish, many of the biographical studies of him are full of such sentimental characterizations as "Noble Norman" and "Socialist Crusader" which distort or obscure the real significance of his life's work through over-romanticization.[2] With Thomas' own request in mind, the following biographical sketch is offered. Hopefully, it will provide insights into the effects of the events in his life on the substance of his writing.

I *Beginnings*

There was little in Norman Thomas' family background or childhood that suggested his future role as one of America's greatest critic-reformers. The eldest of six children born to the Reverend Welling Evan and Emma (Mattoon) Thomas, Norman was reared in an orthodox Presbyterian parsonage in Marion, Ohio.[3] Because he was sickly as a young child, he was encouraged by his exceptionally strong-willed mother to take up reading and intellectual pursuits. As a result, the young man became an avid reader, an activity which he pursued until overcome with nearly complete blindness in the closing years of his life. From the very beginning, the young Thomas read indiscriminately from a broad range of topics ranging from history and literature to popular magazines.[4] By the time he was a teenager, he had outgrown his sickly nature and was able to participate in the normal outdoor activities enjoyed by the Midwestern youth of his time.

Thomas always recalled with a great deal of pleasure what was obviously a happy, secure childhood in a home filled with discipline tempered with love.[5] Speaking years later about his family background, Thomas stated that ". . .my family's standard of morality, while open to criticism from my present point of view. . .was genuinely, and in the best sense, Christian, and disinterested and concerned; and that was the background."[6] Thomas, then, inherited both a deep vein of idealism and a keen sense of responsibility for his fellow man from his family, values that lasted him throughout his entire career. Thomas explained the development of these values in the following terms: "I have been one of the most fortunate among men, because from my childhood I have found security in the love of men and women whose love gave life riches and meaning. From grandparents to my grandchildren I have been blessed in my home. No words can tell what I owe to my wife. From these blessings arise an obligation of service to my fellowmen."[7]

Upon his graduation from Marion High School at the top of his class in 1901, the young man entered Bucknell University at Lewisburg, Pennsylvania. Stifled by what he felt was the unintellectual atmosphere at that institution, Thomas, through the financial aid of an uncle, transferred after one year to Princeton University. Supporting himself by tutoring and a variety of odd jobs, he excelled in debate, history, and politics.[8] At the time of his graduation from Princeton in 1905, Thomas was basically conservative in both his economic and political beliefs. He had read the works of the reformers Henry George and Edward Bellamy, of Frank Norris, and of the Muckrakers at the urging of friends; but they did not impress him sufficiently at that time to cause him to question his conservative Republicanism and his faith in the superiority of capitalism as an economic system.[9]

II *The Ministry, the War, and Socialism*

After graduating as valedictorian of his class, Thomas, seriously considering the possibility of following his father into the ministry, accepted a position as a social worker in a tenement-district Presbyterian parish in New York City. His work among the urban poor played a crucial role in the shaping of his social beliefs.[10] As a social worker, he came face to face for the first time in his life with the brutality, ignorance, and poverty of life in the urban slums. His eventual conclusion that such poverty and human exploitation could not be eliminated from the capitalist system pushed him toward Socialism. Thomas' insights into the nature of human exploitation were also deepened when he accompanied a wealthy friend on a trip around the world in 1907. A considerable part of his trip was spent in Asia where his experiences caused him to become an avowed enemy of colonialism and imperialism.[11]

Upon his return, he became an assistant pastor of another tenement-district church in New York City where he again confronted the brutal realities of poverty. Thomas, convinced that the ministry was his true calling, accepted an associate pastorship at the fashionable Brick Presbyterian Church in 1910; and he began studying theology at the liberally oriented Union Theological Seminary. There, Thomas was strongly influenced by the Social Gospel as expounded in the writings of Walter Rauschenbusch.[12] Thomas' work as associate pastor of the Brick Presbyterian Church caused him to meet and fall in love with Frances Violet Stewart, a young social worker from a prominent New York family. Norman and Violet were married in 1910, and their marriage proved to be a long and happy one. Violet, a somewhat shy person who was troubled throughout her life with chronic heart trouble, bore Thomas six children and created a home filled with love and understanding for him.[13]

After Thomas was ordained in 1911, he assumed the pastorate of the East Harlem Presbyterian Church and the directorship of the American Parish, a federation of Presbyterian churches and social agencies located in the immigrant neighborhoods of New York City.[14] His registration as a Progressive in 1912 and his work for Theodore Roosevelt's candidacy is indicative that urban ministry had pushed him in the direction of more liberal political beliefs. A letter to his Princeton classmates in 1915 provides evidence of the impact of his Social Gospel ministry to the poor on his thinking: "With all my love for Princeton I sometimes think, unjustly of course, that my education really began when I left there and that not the smallest part of it has been the life here in this district. It is a sort of school which sets hard lessons and asks some difficult questions. What is our democracy worth? How shall we apply to our social, industrial and political problems? Are we preparing well for national safety in peace or war when so many of our workers cannot even under favorable conditions make the proper living wage?"[15] Many who read the letter must have been convinced that the Reverend Thomas had found his place in life as a Social Gospel minister to the poor.

The major turning point in Norman Thomas' life occurred when the United States entered World War I in 1917. Unable to reconcile his strong beliefs in the gospel of Christian love and the biblical injunction against killing with the United States government's demand for patriotic support of a "just" war, Thomas became a vocal and active critic of American participation in it. In 1917, he joined the Fellowship of Reconciliation (F.O.R.), an international organization of religious pacifists with strong social-reform tendencies.[16] His activities in this organization included the founding of *The New World* (soon renamed *The World Tomorrow*), the official journal of the group, which he edited from 1918-21.[17] His editorials in this period present detailed evidence of Thomas' increasing disillusionment with the Christian Church because of its uncritical justification and support of the American war effort.

The following excerpt from an editorial in *The New World* exemplifies his disillusionment: "Evidently the doubts the world outside the church holds concerning Jesus as the Lord of battle have not utterly spared our most skillful theologians. Here is a man who bade his followers love their enemies, and pray for their persecutors, who himself died on Calvary opposing wrong by no force save a martyr's death. Him the great body of his church acclaims as Lord and Saviour, the perfect revelation of the divine will, God incarnate. How, then, can that same church justify war in any cause?"[18] Thomas' writing in this period presents a lucid picture of the agonizing struggle of conscience which played such an important role in his transition from minister to radical political activist.

The same hatred of war caused Thomas to support the campaign of Morris Hillquit, the Socialist candidate for mayor of New York City in 1917 who ran on an anti-war platform.[19] Fear that his involvement with Socialists and conscientious objectors would jeopardize the financial support of the American Parish caused Thomas to resign his pastorate that same year.[20] In October, 1918, Thomas applied for membership in the Socialist party and was accepted. His own words about his decision leave no doubt as to his motives: "I came to Socialism for two reasons. First because it seemed to me that only Socialist ideals implemented in a political program could deal with the tremendous problem of poverty illustrated in the East Harlem neighborhood where I then lived and worked as a Presbyterian minister. Second because I supported Socialist opposition to American entry into World War I. I was then a Christian Pacifist. . . ."[21] The Socialism which Norman Thomas accepted was democratic in its scope and content. While he accepted the importance of public ownership of basic industries and services, he refused to accept the Marxian premise that the social order would have to be changed by force.[22]

During World War I, Thomas became greatly alarmed at the violations of civil liberties and at the brutal treatment given to conscientious objectors, such as his brother Evan and other critics of the war effort, by both the government and private groups. This treatment caused him to join other opponents of the war in the formation of the National Civil Liberties Bureau, which attempted to provide legal protection to those opposing the war effort.[23] This organization eventually became the American Civil Liberties Union, and Thomas played a crucial role in its leadership throughout his life.

Thus, World War I was undoubtedly the catalyst which brought Norman Thomas to the major turning point in his life. His reaction to the events of the war propelled him beyond the traditional bounds of the Christian ministry into the realm of social and political activism. There is considerable evidence in his writing, however, that Thomas never fully escaped the influences of his Protestant-evangelical background or his experiences as a Social Gospel minister. His strong sense of conscience, his evangelical approach to politics, his frequent expressions of moral outrage, and his numerous references to biblical and historical parables which appear so regularly in his writing all support this conclusion.[24] Like so many other Americans in this century, the departure of Norman Thomas from the religious orthodoxy of his ancestors did not mean the destruction of his highly developed conscience.

III *Domestic Socialism: The Gospel of Activism According to Thomas in the 1920's and 1930's*

The decade of the 1920's with its Republican normalcy, hyperpatriotism, economic conservatism, and intense nativism presented Norman Thomas with many opportunities to test his newly acquired Socialist faith. Motivated initially by both the economic needs of his growing family and his continuing preoccupation with social issues, Thomas continued his advocacy of pacifism and Democratic Socialism in a series of editorial positions.[25] He was associate editor of *The Nation* from 1921–22. During 1923 he served as editor of the short-lived *New York Leader,* a daily newspaper which the leaders of the Socialist party and its trade-union allies hoped would become the mass-circulation voice of the working class. Despite a high standard of editorial integrity, the *Leader* soon failed because of a lack of finances, the general apathy of the workers who were supposed to form the basis of its support, and the unwillingness of union leaders to support it unless it became a propaganda sheet. The failure of the *Leader* convinced Thomas that it would be necessary for the Socialist party to develop and carry out a massive, long-range educational program to make American workers aware of the need for working-class unity and cooperation.[26] Much of his writing and political activities from that time were directed toward that end.

In 1922, his economic circumstances somewhat alleviated by his wife's inheritance of a trust fund, Thomas accepted the co-directorship of the League for Industrial Democracy, a Socialist organization dedicated to the creation of a social order based on production for use rather than for profit.[27] Supported by a grant from the Garland Fund, Thomas and Dr. Harry W. Laidler, his co-director, worked to expand the League's activities among workers and students. The two teamed very effectively to develop a varied program which included campus speaking, publication of research on industrial working conditions, fund raising to support strikers, and the defense of civil liberties.[28] Thomas' strong belief in the necessity of actively defending civil liberties and his sympathy for exploited workers caused him to participate personally in the picketing and organizational activities of the League in a decade when many Americans regarded such activities as un-American or, at the very least, beyond respectability.[29] On several occasions, as in the bitter woolworkers strike at Passaic, New Jersey, in 1926, his insistence on full civil rights for workers led to his arrest.[30] Active participation in the causes in which he believed and in the organizations to which he belonged was one of the constants of his busy life.

Norman Thomas' keen mind, oratorical talents, and leadership ability brought him to prominence in the Socialist party in the mid-1920's. His nomination and subsequent campaign with Progressive party support as the Socialist candidate for governor of New York in 1924 was the first of a long series of unsuccessful attempts to win public office.[31] He soon became, by his own admission, "a chronic office seeker." Despite his singular lack of success, he was recognized as an enthusiastic and extremely well-informed campaigner who discussed issues rather than platitudes.[32] After the death in 1926 of Eugene V. Debs, the towering giant of American Socialism in its formative years, Thomas emerged as the national leader of the Socialist party. His background and style of leadership contrasted sharply with that of his predecessor, a rough man of the people who left theory to others, who was disdainful of intellectuals, and who regarded himself as part of the working class from which he came.

Thomas ran as the Socialist party's presidential candidate in 1928 and in all of the subsequent presidential campaigns through 1948.[33] Undiscouraged either by the indifference of the American electorate which basked in the warmth of Republican prosperity or by the factionalism in his own party, Norman Thomas in 1928 pushed forward with his plans to plead the cause of Democratic Socialism before the American people. The difficulties which he experienced as a minority party candidate and his struggle to use the Socialist party as the organizational spearhead of a mass workers' party provided Thomas with the evidence for his lifelong critique of the American political system—one of the major themes in his long career as a writer.[34]

Norman Thomas' Socialist convictions, his active personal involvement in numerous reform causes, and his continuous office-seeking were major influences which shaped his writing. Convinced of the need for the publicity of Socialist solutions to the problems facing American society, he became a frequent contributor to such reform periodicals as *The New Republic, The Nation, The World Tomorrow,* as well as to the standard Socialist publications of the 1920's. The themes of his essays reflect his preoccupation with what one contemporary commentator characterized as "social problems and social politics."[35] Covering as they do wide areas of both America's foreign and domestic concerns, these essays present evidence of the wide range of Thomas' reform interests, his firm grasp of the factual and theoretical aspects of the problems about which he wrote, and his confidence in the superiority of Democratic Socialism over capitalism.[36] Even more importantly, these essays graphically portray the close relationship which existed throughout his career between Thomas' activities and his writing. By the end of the 1920's, Norman Thomas' writing was an integral part of his reform personality. Writing from conviction buttressed by experience, Thomas hoped to educate and convince his readers of the worthiness of his goals. His writing may be regarded as a form of secular evangelism, and the volume of his writing is indicative of his faith in its potential for the propagation of his reform ideas.

The stock-market crash in the fall of 1929 brought an end to the Coolidge-Hoover boom years of the 1920's.[37] The ensuing Great Depression brought unemployment, mortgage foreclosures, and a drastically reduced standard of living to millions of Americans. Many who had rejected the Socialist critique of capitalism in the boom years prior to 1929 became convinced of its relevance during the Depression. Indeed, the economic crisis of the early 1930's was an important factor in the temporary revitalization of the Socialist party. Norman Thomas' advocacy of public works projects, unemployment insurance, minimum wage laws, a shorter work week, the abolition of child labor, and general governmental responsibility for the welfare of the economy appealed to many Americans in the lean years of this decade.[38] Many Socialists were confident that the crowds which turned out for Socialist speakers and the 900,000 votes which Thomas polled in his 1932 presidential campaign were signs of even better things to come.

In a letter to Henry Seidel Canby in the fall of 1932, Norman Thomas admitted that his reading continued to be heavily centered upon newspapers, periodicals, and books which dealt with contemporary social, economic, and political problems.[39] Much of his writing was, in effect, his reaction in light of his Socialist beliefs to other people's discussions of what Thomas regarded as pressing social problems. This fact helps to explain the sense of immediacy found in most of his writings. Quite expectedly Norman Thomas' writings of the early 1930's reflect his preoccupation with two topics: the solution to the Depression emergency and the future of capitalism. In four books and numerous articles written in the depths of this economic crisis, he advocated a Democratic Socialist solution to the Depression.[40] In these works, he emphasized the need for the creation of a cooperative commonwealth which would eliminate unemployment by the application of production for use and of long-range planning. He also reiterated his conviction that capitalism was doomed and that it would be replaced by some form of collectivism which he hoped would be democratic in nature.[41]

IV *The Socialist Decline: The Impact of Factionalism and the New Deal*

The brilliant future for Socialism predicted by many American Socialists after their large vote in 1932 failed to materialize. The increased factionalism within the Socialist party over the validity of orthodox Marxist principles and the political appeal of the New Deal combined to weaken Socialist efforts to create a cooperative commonwealth. The emergence of the New Deal intensified the continuing debate over proper tactics which had been an inherent part of American social thought from its beginnings, and thus contributed to the already strongly developed tendency toward factionalism in the party.[42] As might be expected, much of Norman Thomas' writing in the early and mid-1930's was an exposition of his reactions to the two challenges of factionalism and the New Deal. Aligning himself with the "Militant" faction in the party, Thomas rejected the insistence of the "Old Guard" Socialists that the party adhere to strict Marxist orthodoxy. Edward Levinson accurately described Thomas' position in this struggle:

> The elder Socialists, rooted half in a spirit of defeatism and half in a dogma that called for the mere mechanical iteration of their belief in the accuracy of Marxian theory, had begun to resent the aggressiveness of Thomas. He told them he had not left the church in 1918 to join a new one. He told them the class struggle theory was something to be taught as an ideal of solidarity and to be fought for in the day-by-day political and economic struggles. He would not share their feeling that it was to be regarded as a fatalistic scripture of inevitable, unfought for Socialist

victory. . . . With tolerance and hopes of peaceful persuasion, Thomas tried to convince them. This failed for several years and early this year [1936] he performed a surgical operation which has now removed from the party the dead hand of a sterile Marxism.[43]

As noted above, Thomas' writing on Socialist tactics was a call for a pragmatic response to the fast-changing scene of the 1930's. When the "Old Guard" objected strongly to Thomas' willingness to make the party an inclusive one with room for all varieties of Socialist political thought, including the Trotskyites, he found himself alienated from Morris Hillquit and many of his former comrades.

This Socialist split was also complicated by desertions of many younger party members. Some were attracted to the Democratic party because of its spectacular electoral success under President Franklin D. Roosevelt. Others were enticed by Communist attempts to attract the left-wing "Militants" in the Socialist party into "united front" efforts in late 1935.[44] The effectiveness of the Communist appeal enabled the "Old Guard" of the Socialist party to charge that the "Militant" wing was Communist dominated, thus adding to its woes. The debate came to a head in the 1936 convention when the "Old Guard" withdrew from the Socialist party and established a rival group known as the Social Democratic Federation. Two unfortunate factors combined to hasten the party split: Morris Hillquit, the only member of the "Old Guard" leadership who could have brought about a compromise with the "Militants," died in October, 1933; and Norman Thomas' involvement in so many activities outside of the Socialist party gave him too little time to spend in attempts to heal the breach within the party before it was too late.[45]

Even without the intraparty strife which obviously weakened the party's electoral efforts, the Socialist hope of spearheading a drive for a genuine farmer-labor party with Socialist principles was foredoomed to failure because of the impact of the New Deal. The Roosevelt administration stole the Socialists' thunder when, according to Thomas, it ". . .appropriated many measures previously regarded as Socialist."[46] Many former Socialists were convinced that their reform goals would be better achieved from a position of power. Consequently, many younger Socialists, such as Paul Douglas, went to work in the vast array of New Deal agencies created by the Roosevelt administration; others, such as David Dubinsky, assumed places of leadership in the strong coalition of organized labor which supported Roosevelt's New Deal policies.[47]

Not surprisingly, Thomas' contemporary assessment of the New Deal was sharply critical of its shortcomings. Obviously resentful of its appropriation of specific aspects of the Socialist program, he condemned the New Deal's lack of overall conceptualization; and he criticized what he felt was its neglect of basic moral issues in the face of immediate economic problems. Thomas' critique of the numerous inconsistencies of the New Deal remained a principle theme in his writing until it was displaced by his increasing concern with foreign affairs in 1937–38.[48]

It should be emphasized that Thomas' critical stance regarding the New Deal was the product of something far deeper than his frustration over the immediate problems that the New Deal created for the Socialist party. To him, Roosevelt's reforms represented an attempt to forestall the impending doom of the capitalist system.[49] In later years he reassessed the New Deal in much more sympathetic terms: ". . .the New Deal with all its inconsistencies and evasions. . .constituted something like a revolutionary change in American attitudes and politics. It established a welfare state and strengthened democracy."[50] The striking contrast between Thomas' early and later assessment of the New Deal in his writings was the product of a deepened sense of historical perspective which he acquired as he moved farther from the immediacy of the New Deal. Such capability for a different view illustrates the value of his writing as a record of his changing assessments of his reform activities and goals.

V *Defender of Civil Liberties*

Thomas not only continued but greatly expanded what proved to be his lifelong fight on behalf of civil and human rights during the turbulent 1930's. He publicized the plight of the Southern sharecroppers and played a major role in the organization of the Southern Tenant Farmers' Union.[51] His speaking activities for this group in Arkansas placed him in a great deal of physical danger because the enraged farm owners resented his intrusions on behalf of the poor, uneducated, and mostly Black sharecroppers. When the Ku Klux Klan abducted, tortured, and murdered Joseph Shoemaker, a labor organizer in Tampa, Florida, in 1935, Thomas led the attack on the group in Florida which had been responsible for the murder.[52] He was also involved in free speech tests in Terre Haute, Indiana, in 1935 and in Jersey City, New Jersey, in 1938 which ultimately led to the removal of restraints upon basic civil liberties which had been imposed during the unrest growing out of labor disputes.[53]

Thomas' activities on behalf of civil liberties and human rights prompted another of the major themes of his writing in the 1930's. He wrote to arouse public sympathy and indignation over the conditions of both economic exploitation and the suppression of personal liberties in America. In *Human Exploitation in the United States* published in 1934, in parts of his other books, and in numerous periodical articles, he recorded with a great deal of compassion the plight of the downtrodden in American society.[54] Thomas did not stop with the mere publication of these conditions; he used his discussions to argue that the suppression of civil and economic rights were concomitant products of a capitalist society with its emphasis on competition and profits. As he stated in *Human Exploitation in the United States,* "The most that we can say, and indeed the most that is pertinent to this book, is that there cannot be secure liberty for the individual except in a world which has overcome the poverty, the insecurity, and the tyranny inherent in capitalism."[55] His writings on civil and economic liberties were thus an extension of his efforts to educate and persuade the American people that a Democratic Socialist society could better protect basic human and economic rights.

VI *Thomas' Disillusionment with Communism*

The decade of the 1930's saw a hardening of Thomas' attitudes toward Communism. During the 1920's, his reaction to Communism had been marked with some ambivalence. On one hand, he and many other radicals and liberals in the 1920's and during the Depression had been tremendously impressed with the massive economic progress which the Soviet Union had made since the Revolution of 1917 through the development of a planned economy and the self-sacrifices of the Russian people. In this period, Thomas emphasized the notion that it would be hypocritical to condemn Russia without first correcting the evils in our own society such as economic exploitation, violations of civil rights, and militarism.[56] On the other hand, he had never accepted the Communist argument that capitalism would have to be overthrown by a violent revolution. "Salvation by catastrophe," as Thomas characterized the Communist belief, was unnecessary in the United States because the legal means available for peaceful change were readily accessible. This doubt about Communism was reinforced by an even more important one: Thomas and many other Socialists had long condemned the suppression of civil rights which the Soviet Communist party used as it consolidated its power in the Soviet Union.[57]

Direct experience in the 1930's with the disruptive tactics of the American Communist party and careful observation of Communist behavior abroad convinced Norman Thomas that any cooperation between the Socialists and Communists would be disastrous for American Socialism. Earnestly seeking to develop a broad spectrum of radical-liberal support for a genuine farmer-labor party, Thomas and many Socialists had entertained big hopes in the early 1930's for some degree of cooperation with the Communists.[58] Socialist attempts to achieve this cooperation were sorely disillusioned. The Communist party proposals for cooperation with the "Militant" wing of the Socialist party were designed to intensify the "Old Guard"-"Militant" split in the party in the 1930's.[59] Thomas, greatly disillusioned by Communist tactics in the United States, formally rejected all possibility of any organic unity of the American Socialist and Communist parties in 1936.[60]

A trip Thomas made to Europe in 1937 included visits to civil-war-torn Spain and to the Soviet Union. His observations of Communist attempts to dominate the Spanish Loyalist government through murder, torture, and treachery and his firsthand view of Soviet purge trials and slave labor convinced him even more of the incompatibility of Socialism and Communism.[61] "What I saw in Russia and Spain ended any hope I might have had that our Socialist relations with communism could be any other than clear-cut opposition. Socialism is, in its very essence, democratic and communism is totalitarian."[62] In contrast to what some writers have said, the subsequent Nazi-Soviet Friendship

Pact of 1939 only reinforced his already well-developed opposition to Communism.

Norman Thomas' writing in the 1930's clearly recorded his hardening attitude toward Communism.[63] Never an uncritical admirer of the Soviet experiment, his writings reflect a grave concern for the basic immorality and deceit in the behavior of both domestic and foreign Communists. His writing portrays his growing awareness of the dangerous implications of the subservience of the American Communist party to Moscow and thus presents a firsthand account of the factors which caused the bitter disillusionment of so much of the American left regarding Communism in the 1930's.

VII *The Pacifist's Dilemma*

Increasing preoccupation with foreign affairs was clearly the most important force shaping Thomas' writing from 1935 to the outbreak of World War II. His intense hatred of Fascism and his sympathy for the Spanish Republicans after the outbreak of the Spanish Civil War caused him to modify his long-espoused belief in absolute pacifism.[64] As Thomas explained his decision, "I had to moderate my religious beliefs and my pacifism to a degree that I thought of war as an enormous evil—but in some cases a lesser evil than submission."[65] His writing records the mental anguish which this decision caused him.

Thomas' support of the Spanish Loyalists did not extend to those who urged direct American intervention on the side of Britain and France against the Fascist powers when World War II broke out in 1939. Disillusioned by the selfish policies pursued by Britain and France in the 1930's, Thomas became an active supporter of nonintervention through his work in the Keep America Out of War Committee. Mindful of the domestic experience in World War I, he expressed fear that American involvement in a war against Fascism would lead to the suppression of civil liberties and to the creation of a Fascist state in the United States.[66] He reinforced this argument with an additional one against the workability of the idea of collective security propounded by those Americans favoring intervention. In terms which reflected his continuing disillusionment with American efforts to make the world safe for democracy in and after

World War I, he pointed to the selfishness of Britain and France, to their desires to preserve the colonial exploitation in their empires, to the need to keep America as a secure island of democracy, and to the dangers that would stem from American economic involvement on the side of the Allies as arguments against collective security.[67]

Thomas and his fellow Socialists paid a heavy price for their active support of nonintervention in the immediate pre-war period. Because Thomas spoke against involvement on the same platform as members of the extremely conservative and militantly isolationist America First movement, he was accused of being a member of that group. This accusation made him susceptible to the charge that he shared the obvious pro-German tendencies of some of the more reactionary members of that group.[68] This fact and the shift of the American public toward support of the beleaguered Allied cause resulted in the Socialists polling even less votes in 1940 than they had in 1936.

Thomas' writing between 1935–40 reveals his increasing preoccupation with the threat of war. In dozens of speeches, in three books, and in numerous articles, he developed his basic arguments against American involvement. His writing provides an excellent record of the noninterventionist arguments used in the "Great Debate" over American foreign policy which marked the last half of the 1930's. Even more significantly, they reiterate the oft-forgotten point that Thomas was willing to sacrifice his political future for his personal principles.

Writing years later Thomas explained the reasons for his opposition to American involvement: "The success of the blitzkrieg profoundly shook me, but I continued to feel that America lacked the wisdom and power to play God to the world by the devil's method of total war. In the campaign of 1940 I argued—I think correctly—that unconsciously, at least, the drift to war was furthered by the fact that an arms economy was a more successful answer to unemployment than the New Deal had been."[69] This reference to his book, *A Socialist's Faith,* underscores the extremely close relationship between his activities and his writing.

VIII *"Critical Support" of the War Effort*

The Japanese attack on Pearl Harbor on December 7, 1941,

ended Norman Thomas' hope that America could escape involvement in World War II. Shifting to what he defined as a position of "critical support" of the war effort, Thomas gave some indications of the assumptions behind his position in an article in *The Nation* in January, 1942:

> Since the war has become an inescapable fact for us, I have acknowledged publicly the necessity which our government is under to cooperate in good faith with the great nation [Russia] against which Hitler's might appears to be breaking. . . . I have also said that no Anglo-American military alliance which may try to ignore the U.S.S.R. and other nations can succeed in rebuilding the world. Of course I want no future war between such an alliance and Russia, but neither do I want to continue this war indefinitely only to the end that Stalin may become lord over most of Europe and Asia. . . . To me it seems absolutely essential that. . .all of us who believe in democracy should demand more adequate war aims in the Charter of the Atlantic, and give to the German people trustworthy assurances that if they repudiate their dictator, they will not themselves be crushed and their nation divided.[70]

With the above thoughts in mind, Thomas in 1942 founded The Post War World Council, a group dedicated to American participation in a post-war world federation of nations working for peace based on the need for universal disarmament.[71] A fundamental prerequisite for the formation of this organization would be realistic peace terms of a specific nature rather than the much-advertised Allied slogan of "unconditional surrender" and the vagueness of Roosevelt's post-war plans.

Thomas, motivated by his fear that involvement in the war would lead to the destruction of democratic values within the American society, found much to criticize in domestic affairs from 1941–45. He expressed particular concern lest many Americans become "totalitarian liberals" in their haste to defeat Fascism.[72] He was particularly vehement in his condemnation of the removal of Japanese-Americans who lived on the West Coast. When the American Civil Liberties Union leadership hesitated to criticize the government, Thomas threatened to resign and the organization came out with a statement strongly supporting the rights of Japanese-Americans.[73] His statements on domestic or foreign policy did little to enhance his popularity with an American public which regarded Russia as an important ally, "unconditional surrender" as a worthy goal, and domestic security as more important than the civil liberties of minorities during the war years.

There is little doubt that Thomas' position of "critical support" contributed to the continuing decline of Socialist electoral appeal that is reflected in the campaign of 1944. Campaigning on a platform which condemned appeasement of Communism, "unconditional surrender," isolationism, and imperialism, Thomas called for a political peace offensive pledging equal rights to all people and self-determination with organized political and economic cooperation to remove the causes of war. This position was sharply attacked by a wide variety of groups including the Communists, many supporters of the administration's total-victory policy, and a number of Jewish newspapers—all of whom accused Thomas of appeasement, cowardice, and obstruction of the war effort.[74] His 80,518 votes were the lowest total he polled in all of his presidential campaigns. In later speeches and writings, Thomas continued to insist with a good deal of evidence to support his arguments that, had his call for the application of the principles of cooperation and disarmament in 1944 been applied at the close of the war, it might have changed the course of recent history.[75]

IX *An Aging Crusader Keeps the Faith*

American radicalism has experienced sweeping changes since World War II. The same social, political, and economic changes generated by the New Deal, World War II, and the Cold War which created a new tension ridden, status conscious, and permanently insecure American society also created a new style of radicalism; for much of what American reformers had worked for prior to 1945 seemed irrelevant in the post-war era. One of the most significant changes in the radical movement was the development of the New Left, a disparate, youth-oriented, intellectually sensitive, ideologically flexible movement whose principal spokesmen regarded the radical leaders and ideals of past decades with a great deal of distrust. While the New Left has not lost the traditional American radical thirst for the creation of a more economically just American society, the New Left activists and liberal reformers have been increasingly preoccupied with questions of peace and racial justice. Many came to regard the creation of a peaceful world and an open society as absolutely essential prerequisites for the survival of American democracy.[76]

This shift in emphasis helps to explain the growing personal respect for Norman Thomas among radical and liberal elements in the later years of his life. Ironically, these were the same years which saw the continuing decline and eventual disappearance of the Socialist attempts to compete with the major parties at the ballot box. In a very important sense, it can be argued that, during the post-war years, American radicals and, for that matter, a great many more moderate Americans caught up with Norman Thomas. Thomas, from the beginning of his career as a political activist, had preached the message of a Democratic Socialism premised on the creation of a peaceful world and the guarantee of individual civil liberties.

The development and use of the vast destructive power of nuclear weapons and the arms race with its "balance of terror" have caused many Americans since 1945 to seek peaceful solutions to conflicts through the medium of world disarmament, a goal which Thomas had long labored to achieve.[77] The emergence of the Cold War, marked by worsening American-Soviet relations, caused many Americans to accept, though often without much grace, Thomas' thesis about the totalitarian nature of Soviet Communism and the threat it posed to the Western World.[78] Similarly, the struggle of Black Americans for self-identity and political equality which emerged in the still continuing Civil Rights Revolution after World War II caused no problems in theory or practice for Thomas. Painfully aware of the weakening effects which racial segregation had on Socialist efforts in the South, he had long worked for racial equality and for full protection of individual rights for all Americans.[79]

Rapid social change, the arms race, the emerging Civil Rights Revolution, and an increasing fear of Communism—all presented serious challenges to Americans in the post-war period. Norman Thomas, who had been grappling with these complex problems and questioning traditional American responses to them for thirty years, found increased respect for his ideas and activities. It is not surprising that these issues and his personal concern for the decline of organized Socialism proved to be the major themes in his writing during the later years of his life.

Norman Thomas did not permit the infirmities of old age to interfere with his attempt to transform America. The death in 1947 of his wife Violet created a void in his life which even his large and devoted family could never really fill.[80] Neither this loss nor the chronic heart trouble, arthritis, and failing vision which plagued him in his later years prevented his active involvement in literally scores of organizations and activities. Besides his formal affiliation with the Executive Committee of the Socialist party which he maintained until 1950 and the position of its unofficial spokesman which he held to the end of his life, he served at the leadership level in the American Civil Liberties Union, Workers Defense League, The Post War World Council, The Institute for International Labor Research, the National Committee for a Sane Nuclear Policy, Spanish Refugee Aid, and a whole variety of groups operating to secure full civil rights for the Black man and for American withdrawal from Vietnam. Between 1945 and his death in 1968, Thomas wrote seven books, innumerable pamphlets, essays, and newspaper columns; and he continued his lifelong habit of speaking regularly on college campuses in support of the causes in which he believed.[81] His later writing aptly portrays the breadth and intensity of the activism of his later years as well as the new challenges facing American reformers in the post-war era.

And what of his impact? Dwight MacDonald beautifully expressed the attitude of many Americans toward Thomas in his later years after hearing him speak at an anti-war rally in 1966: ". . .we had a special feeling about Norman Thomas, a mixture of admiration, affection, interest, respect, a touch of awe perhaps. It was a pleasure to see him still alive and kicking in 1966, a glorious anachronism, long out of fashion but apparently indestructible. . . . The 'Conscience of America' would be mawkish-pompous applied to anyone else, but as a summary of Norman Thomas it is so accurate as to verge on the prosaic."[82]

The respect shown Thomas in his later years by many Americans proves that at least the prophet, if not his prophecy, can be honored in his own land.

X *Socialism: The Study of Its Failure*

Thomas' writings on Socialism from World War II to the end of his life emphasize two major themes: his continuing advocacy of Socialist solutions to the problems confronting American society and an analysis of the failure of the Socialist party as an electoral force. Speaking at the age of seventy-five, Thomas gave clear evidence of both his own devotion to Socialism and the reasons for his continued faith in it: "Long ago, I stopped believing, if I ever did, in Socialism or socialists as an automatic cure for the ills to which an imperfectly rational human race is heir. . . . What Democratic Socialism must do to some extent is what it is doing today in the name of reason as well as fraternity, that is to challenge us to establish an economic and political order in which plenty, peace and freedom can be natural rather than alien. It is this function of Socialism which holds my loyalty to it in the confusion of our times."[83] Though certainly even less of a doctrinaire Socialist than in his earlier years, it is important to remember that Thomas' Socialism was never of the orthodox variety. He came to Socialism during World War I because it seemed to provide him with a vehicle for the betterment of mankind. His later writing indicates that he never lost his faith that Socialism could fulfill this role.[84]

Not even the demise of the Socialist party could sway him from his faith. As Professor Henry Pelling, the noted British scholar, said of Thomas: "I only met Norman Thomas once but my impression of him—relatively late in life—was that he was maintaining, against odds, a point of view which was already pretty fully established in the 1920's."[85] While his later writing indicates that Thomas was profoundly disturbed and often preoccupied with the decline of the Socialist party under his leadership, it also indicates that he kept his secular faith.

The other aspect of Norman Thomas' writing on Socialism in the post-war period was the result of the continuing decline of the Socialist party as a political force. The process of erosion in the party's power which resulted from the factional splits in the first three decades of this century accelerated in the post-war years. The party—beset by the opportunistic expropriation of its ideas by the two major parties, the loss of its younger adherents to the opportunities for power offered by the liberal wing of the Democratic party, and the continuation of internal factionalization—found itself increasingly less able to make even the pretense of contesting the two major parties at the ballot box.[86]

Thomas, already skeptical about the wisdom of continued Socialist electoral politics, reluctantly accepted the party's presidential nomination in 1948 and ran his characteristically vigorous campaign. Charging that Soviet behavior constituted a threat to world peace, that Henry A. Wallace's Progressive party was Communist dominated, and that the two major parties were too interest dominated to bring about reforms, Thomas polled only 95,908 votes, some 15,000 more than in 1944.[87] His poor showing convinced Thomas of the futility of continued Socialist attempts to conduct national political campaigns against the Republicans and Democrats.

In a move which ran sharply counter to the traditional theory and practices of the Socialist party, Thomas announced that the party should drop its electoral struggle and reconstitute itself into an educational and research unit. Such a move, he was convinced, would lead to a more effective dissemination of Socialist ideas among the American people.[88] Unable to bring the party's leadership to his view and convinced of the need for the emergence of more youthful leaders, Thomas refused to accept renomination to the Executive Committee of the Socialist party in 1950. The Socialist presidential candidates in 1952 and 1956 fared so poorly that the party in 1960 gave up its electoral attempts and reconstituted itself as the Socialist party-Social Democratic Federation and devoted itself to education and research.[89]

Thomas' later writing reflects his preoccupation with the causes of the decline of Socialism in America. Such an analysis certainly provided Thomas with both an apologia for his own role as party leader during the period of decline and the justification for his proposed reconstitution of the party as an educational and research organization. His discussions of the trials and tribulations of Socialism in America should not, however, be dismissed as pure rationalization. His argument that the demise of Socialism in America was the product of events largely beyond the control of Socialists is hard to refute.[90] His own numerous campaigns for public office, as well as his involvement in dozens of causes, gave him a firsthand view of the strength of those forces in the American situation which prevented the political triumph of Socialism.

Advancing age did not lessen Thomas' intense interest in American politics. He remained a persistent critic-commentator on American politics from the time of his last presidential campaign in 1948 to the end of his life. Writing in 1964, Harold E. Fey explained the basis of Thomas' skill on this subject when he noted that: "He has been at the center of creative events for more than 50 years, and because of this personal involvement he has been a remarkably successful interpreter of the political nature of our society."[91] Thomas' involvement combined with his lack of success to give him a singularly unique perspective on American politics.

His calls for ideological parties, higher ethical standards, political courage, and the elimination of racism and graft gave his political writings a highly moralistic tone; but his sincerity always protected him from the charge of hypocrisy. His later writings on politics reflect both his awareness of changing issues and the consistency of his lifelong call for the realization of the full potentialities of democratic principles.

XI *The Cold War: Thomas' Defense of Civil Liberties*

The advent of the Cold War with its threat of Soviet imperialism created new challenges for the civil libertarianism of Norman Thomas. Faced with the dilemma created by the need for individual freedom and national security, Thomas struggled to maintain a viable middle ground that would accommodate the demands of both. As stated previously, he had never been a totally uncritical admirer of the Soviet experiment. His own travels in Russia, the disruptive "united front" tactics used by the American Communist party against the Socialists in the 1930's, and the totalitarian and opportunistic Stalin regime convinced Thomas that the Soviet style of Communism was just as disdainful of human freedom as Fascism. As has been noted, these experiences had destroyed Thomas' earlier hope that the Socialists might develop some type of workable coalition with the Communists.[92]

However, Thomas' hatred of Communism did not cause him to fall victim to the mass anti-Communist hysteria in which so many Americans were caught during the 1950's. The bitter struggle which erupted over the continued membership of Communists in the American Civil Liberties Union during these years made the tension in his beliefs a particularly acute one. His Democratic Socialist faith with its insistence on full guarantees of civil liberties to the individual on one hand and the realization that Communism presented a unique challenge to American democracy on the other caused a crisis in the thinking of Norman Thomas and many other Americans which to this day has not been satisfactorily resolved. Thomas' writing on civil liberties reveals the anguish which he suffered as he attempted to square his civil libertarianism with his conviction that Communism presented a mortal threat to democracy.[93]

As the American people lost a compulsive fear of the Communist menace in the later 1950's, Thomas shifted his attention to what was to be the final phase of his lifelong struggle for civil rights—the Black Freedom Revolution. Thomas lent the full support of his speaking abilities and prestige to the efforts of Black Americans to secure their freedoms.[94] Despite his physical frailty, he was often seen taking part in marches, sit-ins, and demonstrations in both the North and the South during the 1960's. His later writings reflect not only his concern about the polarization of the races which marked American society from the middle of the 1960's on but also his alarm lest the extremist groups in both the white and Black races destroy the chances for the development of the integrated society for which he had labored for so long.[95]

XII *The Search for Peace*

"Since the war, however, my deepest concern has been for peace."[96] With these words Norman Thomas characterized the most persistent theme in his later writings. This statement is not cited to suggest that Thomas was a newcomer to the cause of peace; his interest in the creation of a peaceful world was something which he had advocated during all his public life. He was already a member of the Fellowship of Reconciliation when he joined the Socialist party in 1917 because of its militant anti-war position. Although he had modified the absolute pacifism which he had preached during World War I and the 1920's in the face of growing Fascist totalitarianism during the 1930's, he had never ceased to advocate the settlement of disputes by peaceful means and the creation of a world order based on peace and disarmament. His work, during and after the war, in The Post War World Council, an organization which he founded to preach the gospel of world peace, is ample testimony to Thomas' deep dedication to this cause.[97]

The advent of the nuclear age in 1945, however, profoundly affected Thomas' attitude toward the necessity for peace. Almost alone amid prominent Americans, he condemned the use of the atomic bombs against Japan. He was influential in the founding of the National Committee for a Sane Nuclear Policy (SANE) through which he continued to work from the end of World War II until his retirement from public life in 1967 to prevent the proliferation of atomic weapons through the creation of international controls.[98]

His argument that mankind would extinguish itself unless it found peaceful means to resolve conflicts became the central thesis of his writings on peace in the post-war years. In three books, in numerous articles, and in hundreds of speeches, Thomas preached with fervent desperation that the development of nuclear weapons made the potential dangers of armed conflict intolerable.[99] Writing in 1959, he stated: "Perhaps the greatest change in our lifetime—and this may hold true for all of human history—has to do with the implications of nuclear energy. Atomic weapons, paradoxically, have shattered the institution of the military as a factor in national policy. If we want to serve the cause of freedom, protect the world against aggression, and lay the basis for a better world, it becomes necessary to devise means other than force or the threat of force."[100] To Thomas, the alternatives to the approach which he advocated were unthinkable.

Convictions about the necessity to avoid conflict merged with his traditional Socialist approach to world affairs in such a way as to bring him into sharp conflict with American foreign and defense policies in the Cold War era. Much of his writing was an exhibition of what he felt were the preferred alternatives. Rejecting the idea that world peace could be achieved by a "balance of terror," Thomas criticized an American foreign policy built upon reliance on the production of weapons more destructive than those of the Soviets and the Chinese. Thomas warned that the consequence of the Cold War policy exercised by the United States would be the creation of a "garrison state" which would be dominated by an industrial-military complex with a preference for security over civil liberties.

The stroke which finally removed Thomas from public life occurred in the fall of 1967 while he was in the midst of a speaking tour against American involvement in Vietnam, but even that did not still his pen. Shortly before his death, he finished *The Choices,* a small volume in which he reminded Americans that there were alternatives to the chaos which confronted them. The volume is a fitting summation to the writing of Norman Thomas, for it, like so much of what he had written throughout his life, called upon mankind to live up to its potential. There is no question of the basic consistency of Thomas' love and confidence in mankind.

XIII *Thomas and the American Reform Tradition*

It is necessary, given the modern American penchant to regard Socialism as an alien force, to emphasize that much of Norman Thomas' literary effort can best be understood as a twentieth-century version of the native radical tradition.[101] Nearly all of the values which he espoused were characteristic of that tradition. His passion for social justice, his sympathy for the underdog, his extreme civil libertarianism, his idealism, and his work for the creation of a Democratic Socialist commonwealth are all manifestations of it.[102] There is much in his background that is similar to the patrician reformers who played such an important catalytic role in the development of the American reform spirit in the nineteenth century.[103] His family background, his superior education, and his immense appeal to intellectuals substantiate this point.

Another important argument for placing him in the native American reform tradition can be seen in the manner and style of his activism. Like most earlier American radicals, Thomas emphasized overt, honest dissent; he refused to resort to conspiratorial techniques. He gave graphic evidence of his commitment to this aspect of native American radicalism in a sharply drawn contrast between Communist and traditional radical tactics in America: "To a very considerable degree the Communists have created a problem new in American history because they have deliberately flouted the established practice of American radicals from Colonial times on. That practice was not long-continued secret conspiracy, deceit and concealment, but a flamboyant honesty which, for instance, led the Wobblies of old to fill the jails in towns in which one or more of their comrades had been arrested."[104] Thomas' entire career stands as an example of the traditional American advocacy of open dissent.

Leon Trotsky's remark that Norman Thomas called himself a Socialist "as a result of a misunderstanding" is significant, although not because of its correctness. Thomas' Democratic Socialism was not rooted in the Marxian doctrine of what Thomas liked to describe as "salvation by catastrophe" but in the more idealistic, nonviolent, and democratic variety which had already firmly established itself in America in the nineteenth century. As stated previously, Thomas came to Socialism primarily as "the disciple of events."[105] His immersion in the political and economic developments occurring in early twentieth-century, urban America combined with his already strongly developed sense of commitment to mankind to move Thomas toward the acceptance of a Democratic Socialism which permitted full freedom for the exercise of such traditional American values as equality and opportunity.

It should not be assumed from the foregoing, however, that Thomas developed his Socialism in isolation from his democratic counterparts in Western Europe. His own correspondence, references in his own writings, and his later interviews with the Columbia Oral History Project reflect his awareness of developments in international Socialism.[106] Writing in 1947, he drew a sharp contrast between what he felt were the more nationalist American radicals of the past and the more international-minded American Socialists of this century. Socialism, he was convinced, was an effective antidote to the xenophobia and hyperpatriotism which often marred the native tradition.[107]

There is a good deal of evidence that Thomas' contacts with Western European Socialists played an important, though not controlling role, in the shaping of his Socialist thought. The nature of Thomas' connections with the international Socialist movement were such that they worked to strengthen his already well-developed belief in Democratic Socialism with its emphasis on peaceful, nonrevolutionary change.[108] His writings indicate that such contacts sharpened his perspective about the significantly different position and pattern of development which set American Socialism apart from its European counterparts.[109]

CHAPTER 2

The Techniques of Persuasion

I *An Emphasis on Consistency*

NORMAN Thomas spent his entire public career attempting to persuade his fellow Americans to make basic changes in their way of life. Through prodigious use of both the spoken and written word, he articulated his calls for a cooperative commonwealth based on peace, plenty, and freedom. So great was his reputation as a public speaker in his lifetime that it almost completely overshadowed his reputation as a writer. Many Americans, including this writer, remember with fondness Thomas' passionate calls to action, his incisive wit, and his remarkably persuasive style on the speaker's platform.[1] Few, however, remember as well that Thomas also advocated Democratic Socialism in several hundred articles, in a score of books, in innumerable letters to editors, and in numerous book reviews. If volume is any basis for judgment, Thomas certainly placed a great deal of faith in his persuasive and educational abilities as a writer.[2] Moreover, since Thomas spoke from outlines rather than from textually complete speeches, the most complete extant record of his ideas and the techniques which he used to articulate them appear in his writing.

All Norman Thomas' writing was nonfiction, designed to educate and persuade Americans of the need for action. All of it, including the chapters in his books, was in essay style. Whether one reads his articles or his books, whether one reads his early or his later writings, the reader is struck by the overall unity of the general and specific elements of his writing style. This unity is indicative of the utilitarian nature of Thomas' writing as well as his confidence in its effectiveness. He was most comfortable with the expository essay because it suited his purposes—education and persuasion—throughout his career. The shorter essays were better suited to the constant demands on his time created by his activism. There is no evidence of any sweeping changes in the nature of his writing as he grew older; indeed, the techniques which he used in his articles defending conscientious objection at the beginning of his public career are the same ones found in his book, *The Choices,* which he wrote while dying in 1968. The literary techniques which Thomas found most useful throughout his long career, the manner in which they enhanced the persuasiveness of his writing, and the insights they provide about his reform thought will all be discussed in this chapter.

II *Thomas' Own Thoughts on His Writing*

Norman Thomas wrote little about his philosophy of writing. Most of what he did say about the topic appears in the form of widely scattered remarks in the prefaces of his books; and all of what he said supports the conclusion that he viewed his writing as a pragmatic tool to advance his reform ideas. This view is apparent in his attitude regarding the relationship between facts and bias. He emphasized his determination to state facts fairly while at the same time reiterating his intention to express where his own sympathies lay. Thomas' devotion to factual accuracy is evident throughout his writings. Although he quite obviously exercised selectivity in the presentation of his material, he never succumbed to the temptation to distort it for his own purposes. His faith in the superiority of Socialist values was such that it precluded the possibility of him becoming a victim of such temptations.[3]

Similarly, he ". . .deliberately sought a certain brevity and condensation in the hope of gaining a larger hearing. . ." for his writing.[4] This striving for brevity explains Thomas' extensive reliance on listing to both emphasize and summarize throughout his writings. He applied this listing in a variety of ways to call attention to the principal points in his arguments.[5] Major applications of this technique included: posing a series of rhetorical questions which permitted him to focus quickly on the heart of his topic, summarizing his principal arguments, and separating the various specific points of his arguments into definite categories for the sake of clarification. A typical example was his listing of the three arguments used by American theologians to justify the church's support of American involvement in World War I. This enabled Thomas to develop a clearly organized three-part response which effectively destroyed with brevity the rationale of the pro-war arguments.[6] The use of listing, while contributing a certain monotony to Thomas' style, did make it easier for his readers to grasp not only his major arguments but also the evidence which he presented in support of them. While there is no direct evidence in Thomas' own words to support this view, it seems reasonable to assume that his habit of listing grew out of his earlier attempts to organize his debate material as a student.[7] It underscores the utilitarian emphasis of Thomas' writing; for stylistic matters were all subordinated to the criterion of presenting subject matter in a clear, concise, orderly manner.

His scrupulous care about acknowledging his use of ideas found in current books and journals dealing with economic, social, and political problems indicates both his fundamental honesty and the important role which contemporary thinking played in his writing.[8] This acknowledgment and his repeated apologies to his readers for the flaws in his work resulting from his lack of personal research suggests that he was painfully aware of the inhibiting effects as well as the positive impact which personal involvement could have on the reformer as writer.[9] His admission that most of his books were collections of ideas which he had presented in earlier articles and speeches substantiates the conclusion that his activism limited the time which he could devote to writing.[10] However, that same activism also encouraged Thomas to develop what proved to be one of the most important aspects of his reform writing, his use of the contemporary writings of others as the basis of his discussion of major American problems.

His repeated insistence that he was writing frankly for Americans about the crucial issues facing them also reiterates the pragmatic, contemporary emphasis of his writing.[11] It underscores both the serious intent of Thomas' writing and its American centeredness.[12] Moreover, it explains yet another reason why he used the discussions of contemporary issues of other writers as the basis of his essays. They provided him with a relevant comparative frame of reference in which he could develop his own ideas. The importance of this frame of reference in his reform writing will be discussed later in this chapter.

III *The General Characteristics of His Writings: Realism and Idealism with a Purpose*

An analysis of Thomas' style also underscores its pragmatic and utilitarian emphasis. This quality is apparent in both his general approach to material and in the specific literary and stylistic devices which he used in his effort to convince his readers of the need for changes in American society. Viewed in terms of its general characteristics, Thomas' writing contains most of the elements which typified the Muckraking and Social Gospel writing of the first decade of this century. He combined what his biographer Harry Fleischman described as a "capacity for indignation" with ideas drawn from firsthand experience and from material gained from the writings of others to shape a powerful indictment of the shortcomings of American capitalism.[13] Thomas owes much of the effectiveness of this indictment to the mood of intense sincerity which permeates his writing. He was so obviously sincere that it was impossible to dismiss him as a mere crank or malcontent.[14] That trait and its corollary, an intense concern for one's fellow men, were both significant components of the secular and religious writings of reformers in the Progressive Era.

There is, then, an intensely realistic side to Thomas' writing. He, like both his secular and religious counterparts, hoped to stir the consciences of his readers through the realistic portrayal of the major evils in American life and of the forces which created them. The persistence of Realism in Thomas' writing suggests his continuing faith in its usefulness as a tool of reform. Since the specific examples of the literary techniques which he used to create this Realism are discussed later, the point to be emphasized here is that it remained a constant in his writing because of its usability—a far more important criterion for Norman Thomas than the demands of changing literary tastes.

There was also, as in the writing of the Muckrakers and the Social Gospelers, a definite thread of idealism in Thomas' writing. Thomas, himself, had come to Socialism out of the Social Gospel ministry in the New York City tenements.[15] Though he gave up his religious orthodoxy, his writing proves that he never lost the evangelical style of his earlier career. More particularly, he never lost his passion for saving souls; only the purposes for which he saved them changed.

His later writing reflected the same concern for his fellow men and their earthly problems which had characterized his early career as a Social Gospel minister. His emphasis on the importance of environment in which people lived as the major influence which shaped their lives was the product of his urban ministry.[16] The pleas for Democratic Socialism with which he concluded nearly all of his articles and books were definitely evangelical in style. So also was Thomas' insistence on the tremendous potential of Socialism as a solution to man's problems similar in style to the "good news" message and intent of the New Testament Gospels. One of the best examples of the evangelical style of his Socialism appeared in *A Socialist's Faith:* "If history guarantees us no glowing Utopias, neither does it deny us hope. Men have greatly failed but also they have greatly achieved. There is no salvation without hope. But what can we hope? The socialist tendency has been to offer men assurance of an earthly heaven to persuade them to escape from earthly hells. Heaven cannot be thus delivered or achieved. But a far better society than any men have known is definitely attainable."[17]

Also evident in the idealistic vein of Thomas' writing is an emphasis on freedom of choice which stems from his faith in man's capacity to overcome all of the problems which he faces. So strong was his belief in man's freedom of choice that it led him to entitle two of his books *The Choice Before Us: Mankind at the Crossroads* and *The Choices.* His insistence that man did not have to accept the inevitability of war, poverty, and famine proved to be a continuing theme in his writings. Despite the pessimistic concern for man's future often expressed in his writings, he never lost faith in man's potential ability to save himself from destruction. Numerous examples of his use of the notion of choice resembled his plea in *The Choice Before Us: Mankind at the Crossroads* where he said:

> By no miracle can the next generation be as well off as the last, and that, God knows, was bad enough. We shall either be much worse off or much better. We shall have made our choice perhaps without knowing its fateful quality. We shall rush headlong into the devastation of new world

war and the long agonies of recovery, or we shall have played with the passions, the prejudices, the stupidities and brutalities of Fascism as a prelude to cataclysmic destruction. Or we shall set our hearts and our hopes upon the cooperative commonwealth. We shall use the brains which have given us such marvelous powers of invention to control the things we have made and use them to bring forth abundance. And in sharing that abundance we and our children after us shall celebrate the end of the long night of exploitation, poverty and war, and the dawn of a day of beauty and peace, freedom and fellowship.[18]

There was, then, despite his insistence on the importance of economic forces in the shaping of human behavior, a lasting faith in human freedom of choice evident in his writing. It was certainly one of the most pervasive aspects of his humanistic faith, but its sources also reflect the "free will" aspects of the Protestant Social Gospel theology of Thomas' earlier career.

IV *The Tools of Persuasion*

Examination of the specific literary devices which Thomas used to persuade his readers reveals the paramount position which both direct and implied contrast occupied in his style—the principal means used by Thomas to juxtapose the flaws in contemporary American capitalism with the potential of his Socialist solutions. This strong emphasis on the difference between what is and what could be constituted the heart of his writing; it was the very essence of his persuasive technique. The convincing portrayal of this contrast was the vehicle which Thomas used to create empathy among his readers for his ever-present sense of indignation. It is also the point at which to best observe the interaction of realism and idealism in his writing. The connection between Thomas' writing and his reform personality is thus direct and consistent. His writing was a tool to be used to create a new America.

A superb example of Thomas' use of contrast can be seen in his book, *Human Exploitation in the United States,* in which he compared conditions created by capitalism with their Socialist alternatives: "In so far as, temporarily at least, it is real, there can be no victory for an individual liberty whose champions ally its fortunes to an economic system which has broken multitudes of human beings on the rack of poverty and the wheel of war. The first step in man's final emancipation from a predatory society is to build a system which seeks to share the abundance which already we can create."[19]

Thomas' effective use of contrast was reinforced by his superb sense of irony. He often relied on it to strengthen the mood of contrast in his writing. An excellent example of irony appeared in his early volume, *Is Conscience Crime?*, in which he noted how the very same people who had condemned conscientious objection during World War I were advocating it in the 1920's to oppose prohibition.[20] Another example of his use of irony appeared in his later volume *The Test of Freedom,* where he warned that the United States in pursuit of liberty had given herself ". . .over to an anti-communist hysteria which has all but destroyed her citizens' liberties."[21]

Thomas' precision of description also enhanced his effectiveness as a persuasive writer. Drawing on his varied experiences as a social activist and his extensive reading in current events, economics, sociology, and politics (something which critic Benjamin Stolberg referred to as "simply enormous"), he developed an ability for succinct, accurate characterization which fits in well with his desire for brevity and directness.[22] His writings are replete with versatile description and his treatment of the leading political personalities of this century reflect this skill.

Thomas' poignant, yet incisively critical assessment of Woodrow Wilson in 1921, his moving eulogy of Eugene V. Debs in 1926, and his critique of Al Smith in 1928 provide representative models. For example, there is aptness in his characterization of Debs: "Eugene V. Debs was a leader of men when Bryan emerged. He was the political opponent alike of Roosevelt and Wilson. . . . Uncompromisingly he waged the class struggle. But always he sought for non-violent methods. Gene Debs was a Socialist, but he was also, in the best sense of the word, a democrat. . . . A personality like his lives not so much in some great achievement which poets sing, as quietly in the lives of those who find life better worth living because he has lived."[23] His treatment of the great dissenters in Western civilization in his later book, *Great Dissenters,* also reflects his capacity for brief, clear descriptive characterization.[24]

Both in these studies and in his discussions of issues, he moved quickly to the core of his subject matter. Whether writing about inflammatory, controversial issues, such as the rights of conscientious objectors in wartime or such complex problems as the causes of the Great Depression and the nature of McCarthyism, Thomas' twin canons of absolute honesty and brevity caused him to write with candor. One such example of his directness was his assessment of Franklin Delano Roosevelt in his book, *A Socialist's Faith.* "By his domestic policies in the United States, Roosevelt advanced his country toward a pragmatic socialism; he left a weakened socialist organization in a powerful and bewildered country. By his peace policies or lack of them he made the going for democratic socialism or any constructive substitute unnecessarily difficult throughout the world. Still worse, he greatly aided Stalin's drive for power. It is an insufficient defense of his record to say that some other leader might have done worse."[25] Thomas never left any doubt regarding his position on the issues which he treated in his articles and books.

The colorful phrases and aptness of word selection which added so much to his superb speaking style also enhanced his writing. Such characterizations of Franklin D. Roosevelt as the "Messiah in the White House" during the Depression, of Governor Paul McNutt of Indiana as a "Hoosier Hitler" for his suppression of civil liberties during a strike at Terre Haute, and of capitalism as a "Gambler's Civilization" because of its lack of planning presented definite and relevant connotations to his contemporary readers. Similarly, his reference to New York City politics as being marked by "occasional spasms of reform," his concern lest America "confuse heresy with conspiracy" during the Cold War, his fear because men had not leashed the "wild horses of technology," and his frequent references to the belief of Communists in "salvation by catastrophe" indicate his careful selection of words and phrases to evoke awareness and a sympathetic response in his readers.[26]

Thomas' portrayal of his firsthand experiences added another convincing aspect of realism to his writing. Such activities as his work on behalf of the Passaic, New Jersey, textile workers in the 1920's, his work on behalf of Southern tenant farmers in the 1930's, his contacts with the Communist party, and his lifelong anti-war activities provided him with a deep well of personal experiences which he used effectively to support his calls for the creation of a cooperative commonwealth. One of his most effective uses of personal experience appeared in *The Nation* in 1919 in an article in which he described his encounter with a strikebreaking policeman as a means of showing the violence, bitterness, and ignorance connected with the exploitation of immigrant workers in the United States.[27] This and numerous similar usages helped Thomas create a sense of empathy among his readers, especially because of his indignation about all kinds of injustices.

Another important aspect of Thomas' persuasive writing was his use of current events as an *entrepôt* to the discussion of more significant issues. Working from the premise that it is wise to begin with what is in the forefront of his readers' minds, Thomas frequently used current topics as the basis of a discussion of his reform philosophy. He did not lack interest in the events of his lifetime for their own intrinsic significance, but he was more interested in placing them in the context of a more meaningful framework for analysis, one that would prove truth of his reform philosophy. A typical example of this aspect of his writing was his treatment of American intervention in the Caribbean during the 1920's. He used it to initiate a far-ranging critique of American foreign policy because he felt it violated the rights of smaller nations while it protected exploitative American business.[28] Another excellent illustration appeared in his discussion of the Republicans and Democrats and the political issues of the campaign of 1948 as the basis of his plea for a reconstruction of American politics along more democratic, ideologically consistent, and more responsible lines.[29]

Similarly, Thomas used his discussion of relevant recent books and articles about current events and issues as vehicles to expound his philosophy of reform. He presented his informed critical evaluations of the ideas in these sources to expand and amplify his own interpretation of the topics which he discussed. One example of such usage occurred in his book, *As I See It,* where he utilized a discussion of the writings of Joseph Wood Krutch and Walter Lippman to develop a critique of the state of American society.[30] Both Thomas' books and articles are crammed full of his reactions to such writings, and in some instances these reactions formed the principal basis of narration in his works. Particularly fine examples of this technique appear in Thomas' many book-review essays.[31] While such discussions, seen from the vantage point of modern perspective, seemingly make his work quite dated, they did create a powerful sense of relevance in his writing. They also present the reader with a clear picture of the breadth of Thomas' reading and the process by which he applied it to achieve his reform goals. Education, it should not be forgotten, was a central part of his persuasive technique.

Both the abundance and variety of examples in Thomas' writing point to his faith in their use as an effective persuasive technique. Drawing on his superb education in history, literature, and the Classics at Princeton, his lifelong reading in history, politics, and sociology, and the theological and religious literature of his Social Gospel years, Thomas reinforced his appeals for the cooperative commonwealth with carefully selected analogies which added plausibility and interest to his writing. A great many of those analogies which were historical stemmed from Thomas' lifelong interest in history, both ancient and modern. Although Thomas gave less credence to any notion of rigid historical determinism than he did to an economic one, he did understand and respect the influence which the past exerted on the present. History, to Thomas, did contain many useful lessons, most of which supported his belief in Socialism. Thus, Thomas borrowed freely from both European and American history in his attempt to persuade by example. His use of the failure of Radical Reconstruction after the Civil War as proof that people cannot be coerced militarily and politically to do that which they do not believe in was a typical example[32]—as was his reference to the failure of the Versailles Treaty to prove the difficulties of practicing collective security.[33]

Literary, classical, and scriptural analogies also occupied an important place in his persuasive writing. His continuing awareness of contemporary religious writing in both theology and practical Christianity enabled him to make effective use of scriptural and religious analogies throughout his long career. Numerous references similar to his exhortation of Social Gospel Christians not to leave the church but to stay within as "the righteous remnant" to cure its ills, and his insistence that practicing Christians had ". . .no conception of how completely the Golden Rule is denied by the rule of gold. . ." appeared in his books, essays, and speeches.[34] Such usages were part of his attempt to appeal effectively to as broad an audience as possible, for Thomas made use of what was familiar to many of his readers. They also remind his readers of Thomas' evangelical background and its continued impact on his reform style.

Thomas also made extensive use of literary analogies. His choice of material ranged from classical through contemporary literature. His writing was sprinkled with classical references such as his argument that: "With an insistence greater than that wherewith Cato preached the destruction of Carthage, we must urge that the alternative to the totalitarian state is the cooperative commonwealth."[35] Numerous analogies from more recent literature such as his likening of the results of Fascism to the robots in Huxley's *Brave New World* and his use of Solzhenitsyn's *One Day in the Life of Ivan Denisovich* to portray the horrors of Stalinist concentration camps—also enriched his style.[36] The skill with which Thomas utilized analogy to advance his arguments greatly enhanced both the interest level and the persuasiveness of his writing.

V *The Power of Humor*

There remains one final important aspect of Thomas' writing to consider: why wasn't it marked by the doctrinaire seriousness and dullness which characterized the writing of so many of the left-wing polemicists who were so utterly infatuated with the correctness of their views?[37] The answer to this question lies in Thomas' ability to incorporate his remarkable sense of humor into his writing. This sense of humor, in combination with the variety of persuasive techniques in his writing, prevented the seriousness, intensity, and persistence of his reform pleas from becoming a cacophony of monotony. Because of his willingness to laugh at himself and at his own circumstances, his sense of humor added a touch of convincing humanism as well as a refreshing change of pace. Remarks such as ". . .I would rather be right than be President, but that I was perfectly willing to be both," and his refusal to accept the voice of the American people as the voice of God because ". . .they haven't called me louder despite my urging" are commonplace in his books and articles.[38] Often, he very effectively combined his wit with his strong sense of irony. In one such instance, while discussing his inability to accept his father's orthodox religious beliefs, he said: "I do not believe in his hell, and yet have been sorely tempted to consign not a few thereto!"[39] Thomas used his sense of humor to add both interest and flexibility to his writing. Its persistent appearance throughout his written works suggests that he was fully aware of the dangers involved in taking himself too seriously.

These, then, are the various techniques which Thomas used to convince his readers of the wisdom of his reform goals. Both the general and the specific characteristics of his style of writing point to its use as a pragmatic part of his reform effort. His desire to persuade assured its unity, and it is with the criterion of its effectiveness in accomplishing this purpose that it must be judged. Since the style was an integral part of his reform effort, it reveals much of the essence of Norman Thomas' reform personality.

CHAPTER 3

Creative Socialism

NORMAN Thomas developed three major themes in his writing—peace, civil liberties, and Democratic Socialism. All of his reform efforts were directed toward the creation of a cooperative commonwealth based on their meaningful application. Since the major themes in Thomas' writings were synonymous with his reform goals, his discussions of peace, civil liberties, and Socialism, beginning as they did early in his writing and continuing throughout his career, provide the opportunity to focus sharply on his reform philosophy. Although Thomas articulated this philosophy against the backdrop of the rapidly changing events of five decades, his continuing adherence to the same themes reveals that, despite various significant changes from time to time in his tactics, there was an essential sameness in his reform goals throughout his public life. This inner consistency permits a separate examination of the major themes in his writing and his reform philosophy without doing great violence to either the nature or the intent of his writing.

I *Socialism: The Vehicle for Thomas' Reform Philosophy*

The seminal ideas in all the major themes in Thomas' writings were present in his thinking prior to his conversion to Socialism in 1917.[1] What was missing prior to that time was a sufficiently inclusive, programmatic vehicle for their articulation and implementation. Democratic Socialism provided Thomas with the vehicle to express effectively his humanistic faith. His tactical flexibility, his breadth of knowledge, and his belief in experimentation combined with the libertarian aspects of Democratic

Socialist philosophy to prevent him from becoming a doctrinaire prisoner of Marxist ideology. Instead, his Socialism, largely shaped by the power of his personality, worked as both an organizing and an articulating force for his reform thought. It provided him with a much broader perspective than that held by many of the American radicals who had preceded him.

This examination of the nature and significance of the Socialist philosophy which Norman Thomas advocated so passionately throughout his long life concentrates, though not entirely, on the first two decades of Thomas' career as a Socialist, because that is the period in which he developed and applied his philosophy to most aspects of American life. It provides ample proof that any study of Norman Thomas is ultimately an examination of humanistic values.

II *The Rejection of Capitalism*

The heart of Norman Thomas' Socialism was his rejection of capitalism because of both personal experience and theory. His confrontation with poverty in his urban ministry to New York City's poor immigrants convinced him of its fundamental inequities; the rapidity with which America succumbed to war fever in 1917 indicated that its competitiveness and greed for war markets stimulated the nationalism which led men to war.[2] His conversion to Socialism reinforced his own personal hostility to the capitalistic ethic by introducing him to the fully developed critique of capitalist values. Because the major premise of both his earlier critique and that of the Socialists was essentially the same—that capitalism thwarted the full development of human potential—Thomas was able to synthesize the two sources and create a powerful indictment of capitalism.

Basic to an understanding of Thomas' critique of capitalism is his belief in the criteria of abundance as the basis of his judgment regarding the worth of a society. Simply stated, he believed that it is possible to create a system that can provide for the economic security of all rather than a few of its members. Thomas expressed this belief in the 1920's in the preface to *New Tactics in Social Conflict* when he asserted that behind his work ". . .lies the great belief that man has it in his power to use his scientific and technical skill for his own emancipation and not for his further enslavement to poverty, ugliness, drudgery, suspicion and hate."[3] Later, in the depths of the Depression, he noted: "The basic fact with which any indictment of our social order must start is the presence of bitter poverty in a nation equipped with machinery and resources to create plenty for all."[4] Because capitalism failed to fulfill this criteria or to provide "plenty for all," Thomas believed that it was doomed.[5]

Thomas presented many arguments in the 1920's and 1930's in support of his basic critique of capitalism. He was especially critical of what he termed the "economics of scarcity" which ruled the capitalist competitive system and created "poverty amidst plenty." One of the most revealing expressions of his feelings on this point appeared in 1934 in *Human Exploitation in the United States,* in which he made it clear that not even the humane motives of the New Deal excused it from condemnation because ". . .there has been no great or essential change under the New Deal. Capitalism is still capitalism. It was born of scarcity and under the New Deal it deliberately seeks prosperity by a return to scarcity."[6] The concept of limiting production for the sake of higher prices when people lacked essential materials and goods was totally unacceptable to Thomas. His position on this point is indicative of one of the major causes for his opposition to capitalism—his belief that the basic assumptions of capitalism prevented the fulfillment of man's potential by preventing the creation of an economy of abundance. The existence of any poverty was unacceptable to Norman Thomas; therefore, he never felt it to be a subject which could be treated in relative terms.

Another persistent theme in Thomas' critique was his condemnation of capitalism's inability to use the technology available to it for the common good. Writing in *As I See It,* he pinpointed what he considered to be the crux of this crucial problem when he asserted that ". . .misery is solely due to human failure to manage properly the machinery that might provide for the abundance of all."[7] What was necessary, he insisted, was that machinery be harnessed by other kinds of social control and collectivism than those required by the profit system. He urged the construction of an ethics of technology which would permit its application for the good of the entire society.[8]

Thomas revealed a great deal of fascination and attention in his writing with the impact of technology on modern man. He appeared particularly aware of and concerned with the problem of cultural lag which it had created. In February, 1930, in a review essay of Charles W. Wood's book, *The Passing of Normalcy*, Thomas observed that "The problem is the master of the machinery which forces us all willy-nilly to live in an interdependent and largely collectivist world for which many old loyalties and many social institutions are obviously ill adapted."[9] This and many other references testify to the persistence of his concern.

His awareness of both the dangers and potentials of the new technology reinforced Thomas' conclusion that the crucial point was not its existence, but how it was applied for social purposes—a problem which capitalism had been unable to resolve. Thomas' struggle with the complex implications of technology, "the world the machine made," in the 1920's and 1930's foreshadowed the increasing awareness of Americans today of the results of its uncontrolled growth.

Another important aspect of Thomas' indictment of capitalism was that it lacked the controls, sanctions, and standards necessary to prevent human exploitation and to create human abundance. Capitalism, he argued, was simply too undisciplined because of its insistence on unbridled private competition, on the profit system, and on economy of scarcity. Writing in *America's Way Out: A Program for Democracy* in 1931, Thomas, in reference to George Bernard Shaw's remark that the earth was a "lunatic asylum," urged Americans to examine the principles by which they managed their social affairs because ". . .the trouble may lie in a faulty mechanism of control rather than a hopeless, congenital insanity."[10] Thomas' refusal to accept any determinism which denied man the right to choose his own future is evident.

His objection to capitalism, however, went far deeper than his insistence that it lacked the mere mechanics of control which planning made possible. He was convinced that the charge that capitalism lacked sanctions and controls was essentially an ethical one. The question was, thus, not ultimately one of planning but of the purpose behind this planning.[11] Thomas' continuing emphasis on human choice and on ethical behavior played an influential role in shaping this aspect of his thinking. The Depression gave Thomas convincing evidence that capitalism lacked both the potential to plan and the ability to apply the standards and controls—the ethical judgments necessary to rescue mankind from impending catastrophe.[12] In this area of criticism, as in many others, the Depression provided additional convincing proof which reinforced Thomas' already strongly held anti-capitalist convictions. He was certain that capitalism lacked not only the capacity to plan but also, more importantly, the ability to direct the plan for humanitarian objectives.

Another major aspect of Thomas' criticism, his insistence that capitalist plutocracy constituted a threat to American democracy, had strong roots in the native radical tradition. Just as this concern had formed a major part of the motivation for the writings of such nineteenth-century reformers as Henry George and Edward Bellamy, so did it motivate Thomas and other reformers during the twentieth century. One of his best expressions of this argument appeared in an article in *The World Tomorrow* in 1930 in which Thomas concluded that, "By cajolery and coercion the American plutocracy has gone far toward making American political democracy a disguised dictatorship and still farther toward destroying our older ideals of civil liberty and even of justice."[13] His frequent references to the single tax concept of Henry George as a means of controlling the vested interest of wealth was indicative of both the degree of his concern about the disproportionate amount of power held by the wealthy and of the impact which George's proposed solution had on him.[14] Thomas, like Edward Bellamy before him, saw the disproportionate power and status possessed by the wealthy in American capitalist society as a serious threat to the broad range of liberties due Americans as their birthright. Reinforced by observations during his day-to-day reform activities, this threat was very real to him.

Capitalism possessed what to a dedicated pacifist was an even more telling defect. Moved by the same definition of the causes of war which had been one of the major reasons for his conversion to Socialism during the First World War, Thomas insisted that the competitive aspects of capitalism and its lack of internal controls placed it in a position where it was ". . .compelled to accept war. . .or is impotent to avoid it" as an inevitable part of human relations.[15] During the 1920's, with the memories of the war fresh in his mind, he relied more heavily on his old anti-imperialist assumptions as the basis of this charge. Writing in *New Tactics in Social Conflict* in 1926, Thomas developed this aspect of his charge by illustrating the connection between imperialism and capitalism.

He did so by emphasizing that modern, vigorous, imperialistic foreign policies were the consequence of two causal forces: first, the large surpluses in the hands of domestic capitalists caused by the denial of the just fruits of their toil to workers; second, the demands of raw materials from all over the world, the acquisition of which exploited the workers in the countries producing the resources. Noting that such an imperialist foreign policy buttressed the profit system at home by providing at the same time markets and sources of raw material, Thomas concluded caustically: "It is therefore a defense for capitalism—the kind of defense, however, which ultimately is likely to mean catastrophe not only for the system but the men and women who must endure new wars born of an imperialist policy."[16] Thomas was convinced then that war between clashing capitalist imperialisms was inevitable, and his desire to avoid such holocausts explains the sense of urgency in his Socialist message.

Another aspect of capitalism which Thomas felt led to war was its close tie with nationalism. The amoral drive for power which formed such an important part of the national state had combined so completely with the will for profit that the system was beyond redemption. Writing in 1934 in *The Choice Before Us: Mankind at the Crossroads,* he said: ". . .man's worship of his twin gods, the Golden Calf of private profit and the Moloch of the absolute national state, has cost him both the will and the intelligence to do what theoretically might have been done to prolong the life of a relatively secure and peaceful capitalism."[17] To Thomas, the irrationality of capitalism and of nationalism reinforced each other and placed another insurmountable obstacle in the path of those who maintained that capitalism could be reformed. He cited as evidence the Versailles Treaty which, he argued, had thrown capitalism out of balance, stimulated new nationalist rivalries, and increased hatred between nations.[18]

The rise of Fascist military dictatorships in the 1930's provided Thomas with additional evidence that capitalism in conjunction with nationalism led to war, something Thomas was already convinced of because of his experiences during World War I. "Fascism," he insisted, was "the evilest spawn of capitalism and nationalism, of the acquisitive society and war."[19] The close relationship that he saw between capitalism, nationalism, and Fascism received increasing emphasis in his writing in the 1930's. It provided Thomas with an emotionally charged, relevant means of expanding his indictment of capitalism.

The foregoing defects led Thomas to one conclusion: capitalism was incapable of redeeming itself by internal reform because its practitioners lacked both the desire and the ability to reform the system from within.[20] This fundamental defect meant that it would have to be replaced by a new system which would be free of the evils of the old. An examination of the reasons why Thomas felt that Democratic Socialism was such a system is in order.

III *The Transition to Socialism: The Concern for Peaceful Methods and Civil Liberties*

One of the most recurrent themes in Thomas' writing in the 1920's and 1930's was his discussion of the proposed transition from capitalism to Democratic Socialism. Like Edward Bellamy who preceded him, his insistence that the transition be a peaceful one in which civil liberties were preserved stemmed from the consistent application of his own personal beliefs in civil libertarianism and pacifism to his political theory. It illustrates the controlling influence which these two aspects of his personal belief played in the shaping of his Socialism. This view of a legal evolution of a new society underscores the contrast between Thomas' conception of revolution and that of the Communists and other radical groups of the period. His emphasis on nonviolence was typically American and clearly illustrates the influence of the native liberal reform tradition on him.

Advocacy of a peaceful transition to Socialism appeared very early in Thomas' writings, and it was particularly evident in his numerous discussions of the problems of labor organization in the first decade of his Socialist career. Writing in *The Nation* in October, 1919, he asserted: "Labor unions have plenty of faults, but one hope of comparatively peaceful social readjustment is in the growth of responsible industrial unionism as opposed to bitter and irresponsible 'mass action.' "[21] One of the major reasons then for his support of unionization was his view of it as a vehicle for nonviolent change. His writings reflect a considerable amount of chagrin because the enemies of labor organization did not realize that frustration of its intent would inevitably lead to the violence so many of them feared. Nonviolence for Thomas was far more than a theoretical position; it was a principle which he attempted to apply in all of his activities.

Not even the increased sense of desperation and the intense economic wants suffered by his fellow Americans in the Great Depression could shake Thomas' faith in the efficacy of a peaceful transition from Socialism to capitalism. This view was apparent in his discussion of the concept of the class struggle during the 1930's. In a letter which appeared in *The World Tomorrow* in 1932, Thomas noted:

> I believe that the class struggle is one of the inescapable facts about human life in our present stage of capitalist organization. With all my heart and soul and mind and strength I desire a classless society in which there will be no more class struggle. Socialists in recognizing the existence of the class struggle do not mean that they like it. You cannot, however, get rid of the struggle by burying your head in the sand and denying that it exists. . . . I wish to substitute other methods than the methods of war in carrying on this essential struggle to the end of the abolition of the class division in society. This is in line with my general opposition to the war method.[22]

Much of Thomas' concern about nonviolence was the result of his belief that violence begat violence—that it was counterproductive. This conviction was evident in his frequent contrasts of Socialist and Communist tactics in the 1920's and 1930's. Thomas stated his basic objection to the Communist position in a 1921 article in *The World Tomorrow* in which he assessed the status of radicalism in America: ". . .it is hard to be enthusiastic over the coming of chaos in the hope that the survivors, if any, can establish Communism."[23] He repeatedly condemned the Communist advocacy of class warfare and violence as belief in "salvation by catastrophe."[24] He expressed fear that it would lead to a Communist party dictatorship, the antithesis of human freedom. As evidence in support of his argument, he cited the disregard of human rights which marked the rise to power and the current behavior of the Communist party dictatorship in the Soviet Union.[25] The willingness of the Communists to resort to any means including violence, deceit, and treachery to achieve their ends placed them outside the bounds of ethical decency which Thomas regarded as an important part of his democratic approach to Socialism.

Just as the transition to Socialism was to be nonviolent, so also, according to Thomas, was it to be one in which civil liberties were preserved. Writing in *As I See It* in 1932 in a chapter appropriately entitled "Liberty's Hard Road," Thomas posed an important question: ". . .how will liberty fare in a world somewhat painfully adjusting itself to the necessary collectivism of a machine age?"[26] Thomas, who addressed himself to the question in good Socialist fashion, noted that any man would gladly exchange his theoretical liberties for economic security, that actual living conditions in capitalist society had made liberty more or less of a special privilege of the few, and that freedom for the poor quite often only meant the right to be taxed and conscripted.

Was Thomas here building a sly case for the subordination of civil rights to economic security? Is this not a political justification for totalitarianism in the guise of granting economic security? Actually not. His point in *As I See It* and in numerous other places in his writing was one which reformers, like Edward Bellamy and Henry George, had suggested before him: economic security is in itself a fundamental civil right, one whose presence goes a long way toward assuring not only the continued existence but the expansion of other civil rights.[27]

Having thus criticized capitalist society for its failure to provide the security necessary for the full enjoyment of his broadened concept of potential human liberties, Thomas expressed his own strong belief in the need for not only a continuation but an expansion of civil liberties during the period of transition to the Socialist commonwealth. He emphasized that the preservation of dissent was for the common good of mankind because ". . .heresy has been the growing point of society."[28]

IV *The Challenge of Fascism*

The rise of Fascism with its adoration of violence and its sacrifice of personal freedom for the glory of the state also influenced Thomas' discussion of the nature of the transition from capitalism to Socialism. The continuation of Mussolini's power in Italy, the emergence of Hitler in Germany, and the Fascist revolt led by Franco in Spain in the 1930's created an awareness in Thomas of the mortal threat which Fascism posed to Democratic Socialism. His writing reflected his growing conviction that the transition to Socialism hinged on the successful outcome of a struggle between Fascism and Socialism for the minds of men.[29]

Thomas' study of both Communism and Fascism led him, therefore, to become much more cautious in the middle and later 1930's than he had been previously about the nature of the transition from capitalism to Socialism, for he recognized that the movement toward collectivism which he regarded as an important part of the historical process did not automatically guarantee that it would be Socialist or democratic. Writing in a 1938 issue of *The Social Frontier,* he discussed in detail the problems confronting those who would transform America into a Socialist state:

> Broadly speaking the socialist problems can be reduced to two which are basic:
>
> 1. Under what sort of machinery and by what sort of plans can production for the use of all be established without the evils inherent in the totalitarian state under a dictatorship? What would a socialist society look like?
>
> 2. How shall we be able to make the transition from a capitalist to a socialist society? Must it be the product of war and violence? If a socialist state in the making must protect itself by militarism how can it escape the consequences of militarism?[30]

That Thomas raised such questions is proof of his increased awareness that the problems of transition from capitalism to Socialism had been greatly compounded by the rise of totalitarian states. The Communist and Fascist use of highly centralized governments as instruments for violence and the repression of civil liberties created reservations in Thomas' thought about the use of government centralization to advance Socialism.

V *Building Socialism: The Basic Generalizations*

"In its broadest sense Socialism is the doctrine that land, natural resources, and the principal means of production and distribution should be socially owned and democratically managed so that production should be for public use rather than for private profit."[31] With these words, Thomas presented a succinct definition of what he regarded as the essential features of Socialism as an economic system that would guarantee and preserve America's basic principles. Thomas' attempt to achieve a way of life embodying these beliefs was the motivating force behind his lifelong written exposition of Socialism. He addressed himself in this writing to two questions: first, who would build Socialism?; second, how was it to be built? From the time of his conversion to Socialism in 1917 through World War II, he articulated answers to the two questions that were remarkable for both their consistency and the confidence with which he presented them. In so doing, he presented a vivid picture of a reformer attempting to articulate a believable, pragmatic means of transferring theory into reality in the face of heavy odds.

The nature of his discussion of who would built Socialism underscores the inclusive, nondoctrinaire nature of his faith. He rejected the traditional Leninist concept that revolution would come as the result of a revolutionary elite which would direct a landless industrial proletariat because of its lack of relation to American realities and because it was predicated on violence. In the place of the proletariat as a sharply defined entity, he insisted that the "workers of hand and brain" would lead the transition to Socialism. A clear description of how he defined this term appeared in a letter which he published in *The World Tomorrow* in August, 1932: "This will be done by the organized effort of the working class, and in the working class I include all those who do an honest day's work with brain or brawn, in farm, mine, factory, school or office."[32] Thomas' definition made membership in the working class less dependent on occupation and more on the individual's assessment of the worth of his economic activity.

As Thomas emphasized in the same letter, he was not naive about the practical difficulties that would confront the Socialists as they attempted to articulate this larger concept of class consciousness: "Unfortunately, a great many workers do not recognize themselves as workers or permit themselves to be divided by relatively minor interests so that they do not assert their real solidarity. . . . The ideal of class solidarity is ethical even though it conforms to the deepest economic reality; it is something that must be taught."[33] The inclusiveness which Thomas desired explains the importance of education in his approach to Socialism.

Thomas had insisted as a clergyman that the good

tidings of the Christian Gospel were for all who heard it, and his approach to Socialism was the same. The very inclusiveness of his "revolutionary class" turned the concept of class warfare on its head and emptied it of its traditional Marxist meaning. The creation of Socialism would be the product of open organization, and the emphasis would be on the inclusion of as many groups of Americans as possible. American Socialism, as defined by Thomas, would not fail because of either its secrecy or its exclusiveness. Principle and pragmatism merged with ease in this aspect of his Socialism, and his intention to absorb rather than to destroy the middle class is apparent.

Thomas' plan for the creation of a Socialist commonwealth was a twofold one which emphasized the need to develop and apply general principles and a definite plan of action. Of the general principles, two—the importance of reason as an analytical tool and the necessity for Socialist education—stand out in his writing. In both cases, the manner in which Thomas treated them underscores the close relationship between theory and practice in his concept of Socialism. Indeed, his insistence that man could solve his own problems by the application of human reason is one of the most frequently recurring themes in his writing; for, as previously stated, it quite often manifested itself in the context of the discussion of choices open to man.[34] Writing in *Scribner's Magazine* during the Depression, he expounded on the use of reason in building Socialism: "Diagnosis must come before prescription. . . . To reach that harbor requires the creative energy of the informed human will."[35] Reason provides man with a means of understanding both the nature of the problems troubling him and the means necessary to overcome them. Reason, when reinforced by both knowledge and the desire for change, is a powerful tool for human betterment. The emphasis upon reason explains Thomas' confidence in planning: planning is reason made manifest.

The second general approach to building Socialism which Thomas emphasized in his writing was Socialist education, a natural extension of his faith in reason. The heavy emphasis on this means of building Socialism in his writing during the 1920's was the result of his involvement in the League for Industrial Democracy whose primary goal, it will be remembered, was dissemination of Socialist ideas among workers and students and the creation of cooperation between workers and intellectuals.[36] Consequently, the emphasis on education as a means of making people aware of the need for Socialism was more clearly formulated in the first decade of his career as a Socialist than a number of other aspects of his political thought.

One of the best expositions of what Thomas envisioned as the specific nature of Socialist education appeared in a long letter in *The New Republic* in 1923. In it, Thomas stated his belief that education was a pragmatic tool, "a legitimate instrument," of emancipation that would free the worker and bring an "end to class divisions."[37] It is important to remember his inclusive definition of the working class at this point. Continuing, he expressed admiration for the statement formulated by the Belgian workers' educational movement describing the goals of Socialist education: "To instill into the workers the knowledge and the qualities which fit them for carrying on the struggle for the emancipation of their class in every sphere."[38] Thomas' definition of Socialist education was conditioned by his faith that Socialism would triumph and by his concern that its practitioners should be prepared to accept the responsibilities of power. The impending assumption of such awesome responsibilities could not be left to chance.[39]

Just as important as the ultimate application of this kind of education was its use as a vehicle to build Socialism during the period of transition between capitalism and Socialism. As Thomas asserted in *The New Republic* letter, "Education as a social process is bound up with social action. Education either lifts the workers out of their class or enables them to be more effective in their class for its emancipation."[40] To reinforce his point, Thomas related how he had recently returned from a coal-mining district in which the workers had lost a strike because, in part, such education was lacking: "Workers in that district need education. They need to live in the 'shadow of truth'—I should prefer truth to its shadow—but to say that truth is independent of class conflict is to make truth an empty thing. Education of those workers means a training in the better selection of their own leaders, a fuller education of themselves and their leaders for the difficult tasks on hand. It means thought on the fundamental question whether coal belongs by right to absentee owners or to society."[41] As is apparent from this statement, Thomas regarded education both as a practical tool to attack the immediate problems which the workers faced and, more significantly, as a means of questioning the entire capitalist system of ownership.

Thomas completed his discussion of workers' education in his *New Republic* letter with a discussion of whether such efforts were really education or propaganda. He began by drawing a sharp distinction between the two: "The difficulty as we conceive it between education and propaganda is not that the educationist has no opinion, no program to impart, but that he is careful to impart it on the basis of fact and to ask the cooperation of those whom he teaches in getting the facts and working out a theory."[42] Education was not, to Thomas, a neutral process without human value judgments; it was the active advocacy of factually sound value judgments proven by experience. For those who feared that his concept of education still smacked of propaganda, Thomas related the following story of an event which had occurred at an English conference a number of years before: "An American woman hung in reverence upon every word that fell from the lips of G. B. Shaw. At the conclusion of the conference in a sketch taken of the events of the conference, she was represented as saying, 'Oh! Mr. Shaw. How I love that man! He is the man that made me think.' 'Think, think what?' 'Think? Oh, nothing in particular, only Wonderful, Beautiful, Eternal, Thought, Thought, Thought.' "[43] Education devoid of content and purpose and unrelated to improving man's position was an anathema to Norman Thomas.

His continuing advocacy of the kind of education which he defined in this early letter to *The New Republic* indicates that he maintained his beliefs about the pragmatic nature of Socialist education. For example, when faced with the reality of an American labor movement which, he felt, had been seduced by the reform capitalism of the New Deal in 1938, he emphasized the necessity of educating workers so that they might desire something better.[44] Similarly, he felt in that same year that American involvement in war could be avoided if Socialists would ".. . .educate and organize the workers. . ." in the need for peace.[45] Thomas' faith in education played a critical role in the major transition in his tactics after World War II.

CHAPTER 4

Building Socialism

I *The Three Interrelated Essentials of His Plan of Action*

THE specific plan which Thomas advocated for the building of Socialism consisted of "...three indispensable things in the forward struggle of mankind, ..." a philosophy, a program, and an organization.[1] Most of his writings about Socialism contain, therefore, expositions of one or another aspects of this plan. Collectively, they present convincing evidence of the basic consistency of this aspect of his thought during the first three decades of his career as a Socialist.

A proper philosophy was essential to Thomas' Socialism. Writing in *The World Tomorrow* in 1930, he explained why: "Socialism has the immense advantage of offering an ideal, a philosophy of social control and the dignity of labor which even in its least dogmatic form is one of those great generalizations by which...men live."[2] Philosophy, to Thomas, was much more than a rationalization for doing something to an economic system: it was an explanation of a new way of life and the guide which would carry men from capitalism to Socialism. He never permitted it to degenerate into a dogmatic creed, a set of static principles to which he might become enslaved; and warnings against such dogmatism recur frequently in his writings.[3] Thomas' philosophy articulated his belief in man's ability, given the right economic and social conditions, to achieve peace, plenty, and freedom.

Another important aspect of Thomas' philosophy was his insistence that it be adequate for the times.[4] Especially important in his thinking was the criterion that it be relevant to the two major directions in which he felt society was moving; consequently, he emphasized the importance of a Socialism which considered the ever-increasing impact of technology and the definite movement toward collectivism in modern industrial society.[5] These two tendencies provided both opportunities and problems for those who would build Socialism in America.[6] Thomas was convinced that "social control" supported by planning provide the necessary approach to deal humanely with collectivism and technology.

The primary argument in Thomas' discussion of planning —his insistence that it be related to the right purpose—illustrates his determination that it be used for Socialist purposes. Writing in a 1931 issue of *The New Republic,* he stated that ". . .no one is more fully persuaded than I of the necessity of planning. But the first step in curing our sick society is not plan, but purpose. The truly revolutionary decision concerns not the kind of planning commission we shall set up to harness the 'billion wild horses' of a machine age, but whether we seriously intend that they shall work for the use of all of us rather than the profit of private owners."[7] Planning, he insisted, was only worthwhile when it was directed to such ends that would create a system for the benefit of all. As a result, any plan conceived had to be dependent on proper ethical assumptions.

Assuming that a decision was made in favor of planning for the use of all, what kind of actions would be necessary in order to permit the kind of planning essential to the creation of the new society? Thomas wrote extensively about what he regarded as positive planning—that dedicated to the application of technology for the good of all. Such planning would be impossible, however, unless society controlled that which it planned for on a permanent basis.[8] Success would only be possible with the development of a social consciousness that accepted this reality.

The necessity of "positive planning" thus convinced Thomas of the logic of public ownership. One of his most impassioned pleas for public ownership as the basis of planning appeared in the October 7, 1931 issue of *The Nation*:

> Why not, then, be candid enough to face the facts which by implication we have all admitted? Why not accept the logic of public ownership of things necessary for the common life? There will still be difficult questions to answer. The new social order will have to be experimental. It cannot be established overnight. But it cannot be established at all unless we have some compass to steer by and some conception of the goal we

want to reach. These are things that doom to ultimate failure any scheme for plastering plan on the essential planlessness of the profit system.[9]

Planning and public ownership were principal parts of his attempt to apply his Socialist philosophy to the realities of the situation which confronted him in the 1920's, 1930's, and 1940's. Both rested on and were motivated by his faith that capitalism was giving way and that some form of collectivism would replace it.

The faith which Thomas placed in proper planning and in public ownership did not blind him to the defects which might accompany them. One of his most comprehensive discussions of the problems surrounding economic planning appeared in *As I See It* in 1932. After reiterating a number of points about planning which he had made before, Thomas raised two questions about the relationship between Socialist planning and human freedom: First, can planning coexist with political democracy? Second, can planning on an effective scale leave some range of consumer choice?[10] Regarding the first question, he admitted that, while he could not answer with certainty, he did believe that planning under democracy would succeed ". . .in proportion as the democracy is committed to the philosophy of socialism and to the necessity for intelligence in operating it."[11] Thomas was confident that such a democracy would be one which emphasized a "general interest." It is apparent from his comments that he did not believe that Socialism furnished a precise, automatic answer to the problems that would arise from relating planning to liberty.

Regarding the equally complex second question, the relationship of planning and consumer choice, Thomas became much more specific. He thought that hope for the success of such planning resided in three things:

1. The possibility of learning the average tendency of consumers' choice and even educating it. . . .
2. . . .the productivity of machinery allows for a very considerable amount of waste from an abstract standpoint without breaking down the system; and
3. . . .workers can be guided by information and induced by differential rewards to take the necessary jobs.[12]

Although optimistic about these possibilities, Thomas was apparently not convinced that Socialism would automatically assure the

success of these hopes anymore than it could guarantee the nature of the relationship between planning and liberty. Socialism would have to be developed and applied pragmatically to the American scene. He realistically anticipated a number of the problems of adjustment that such a transition would create. Thomas' philosophy provided an outline for his Socialism; but, more than that, it caused him to think seriously about many of its details.

The detailed program which Thomas developed from his philosophy first appeared in his writings on Socialism in the depths of the Depression, and it remained virtually unmodified until well into the post–World War II era. One of the most succinct expressions of this program appeared in an article in *The World Tomorrow* in February, 1930.[13] In it, he listed four proposals which he regarded as essential to the creation of a Socialist program in America.

> 1. The preservation and increase of civil liberties, including the right of labor to organize, strike and bargain collectively.
> 2. War against insecurity and poverty by social insurance against old age, sickness, and unemployment, by a nation-wide system of employment exchanges, by the use of public works. . . .
> 3. Socialization of key industries and services beginning with those in which already the engineer is more important than the entrepreneur. These would include public utilities, especially the power industry, coal mining, banking. The form and degree of social control might vary. In every case administration should be non-political or functional. . . .
> 4. In order to provide money for increased governmental service and to aid in a more equitable distribution of wealth, taxation should fall principally on land values—which society should take since it creates them—income, and inheritances. . . .[14]

The first two points relating to civil liberties and social insurance were applications of Thomas' twin beliefs in the primacy of civil liberties and his hope that they could be broadened to include the right of economic security. They also reflect how favorably impressed he was with the social-welfare systems developed by European Socialists as well as with the strong sense of responsibility for his fellow man which was the result of his earlier Social Gospel career. His third point on socialization is traditional, but it contains a bow of deference to Americans who feared that it would lead to bureaucratic excess. Thomas' fourth point was a direct expression of the old native radical fear of plutocracy. The suggested taxation of land values was an application of the single-tax concept of the nineteenth-century American reformer, Henry George. Traditional American radical thought and Socialist thinking merged with ease in his program.

Just as Thomas' program was an attempt to implement his philosophy, so was his work for organization an attempt to implement his program. Thomas devoted the final part of a 1930 article in *The World Tomorrow* to the problem of how to implement the program which he had proposed. He was convinced that the entire matter of implementation hinged on Socialist success in another crucial area: "That is organization. Such organization, as I have indicated, cannot be solely political. It must include labor unions, farmers' organizations, consumers' cooperatives. Indeed, every sort of organization great and small must minister to the new social attitudes if our purpose is to be achieved. But in America there is peculiar need for a party with a philosophy and a program of service to the Socialist ideal."[15] Organization proved to be a critical area of concern for Thomas, for no Socialist program could possibly be successful unless it was implemented through the coordinated effort of numerous organizations. Thomas' frequent discussions of the need for strong unions, cooperatives, and a Socialist political party emphasized his belief that success was dependent on the coordination of economic and political action.[16] His continuing discussion of the problems of organization suggests that he was fully aware of the staggering challenge that confronted him.

The challenge of union organization for Socialist purposes absorbed much of Thomas' attention during the first two decades of his career. This period, the 1920's and 1930's, was one of high hope that organized labor would transcend its place within the capitalist system and its traditional support of two-party politics and embrace Democratic Socialism through the development of an independent industrial union movement. Thomas' writings on organized labor during this period were basically expositions of the way he hoped this situation would develop.

One of Thomas' most incisive discussions of the potential of labor organization as a means of building Socialism appeared in the January, 1925, issue of *The World Tomorrow*.[17] He opened the essay with a discussion of worker solidarity which underscored his belief that the growth in this aspect of behavior was necessary to build Socialism: "The soul of this struggle has been a glorious sense of solidarity. Under its operation men, women and children have endured almost incredible privation for the sake of the cause without breaking ranks. With extraordinary sense of equality they have divided among them such meager resources as they possessed. Leaders, many of them unknown even to the labor historian, for the sake of their comrades have been blacklisted, persecuted, imprisoned."[18] Thomas saw in this aspect of worker behavior the same willingness to keep the faith and sacrifice for a cause which had been present in the early Christian Church.

Thomas' advocacy of labor organization and the appeal of labor solidarity to the idealistic aspect of his nature did not blind him to the defects in the labor movement. He cited such things as the decline in union membership and the disturbing tendency of major labor leaders to spurn independent political action in favor of positions inside the old parties alongside the men who had threatened working-class voters in the last election with a loss of jobs if they voted for Robert La Follette.[19]

Thomas expressed special concern about the need for effective and experienced leadership, and he presented an incisive discussion of the pitfalls inherent in its development:

> Yet it is very hard for the leader to keep in vital touch with his own rank and file. Responsibility makes him conservative. . . . Labor unions carry no charm against bureaucracy nor is the labor leader proof against autocracy and snobocracy. . . . To hold one's post becomes too often the chief end in life for the labor official who, having tasted power and enjoyed a relatively high income, has no desire at all to go back to the old job in the mine or the clothing factory. . . . No wonder, therefore, that it is a rare labor leader who will favor actively the amalgamation of his trade union into an industrial union, when it may mean the loss of his job. That fact is one, though not the only one, of the difficulties in the way of the development of industrial unionism to meet modern conditions.
>
> The desire for office and power has resulted in some unions in most undemocratic constitutions.[20]

Thomas was certainly aware of the complex ethical problems associated with labor organization.

As for what Thomas thought about labor's chances of overcoming the problems he had cited, he was generally optimistic because they were "...perhaps more or less to be expected in the rough and tumble first stage of labor organization."[21] Writing in the springtime of his Socialism, Thomas can be forgiven for not realizing that the problems which he regarded as transitory were actually endemic. Many of the same problems which he observed in their nascent state in the 1920's still troubled American labor fifty years later. Settling as labor did for a secure power position in a reformed capitalist economic structure, it never achieved what Thomas hoped would be the Socialist phase of its development. His aspirations for the role it would play in building the cooperative commonwealth were to be stillborn.[22] His later writings on organized labor reflect his sharp disappointment at what he felt was labor's unwillingness to live up to his aspirations for it.[23]

The second type of potential Socialist organization which Thomas discussed was the cooperative, a form of organization that had traditionally appealed to the Socialist because of its emphasis on effective distribution, group purchasing power, self-government, cooperation, and planning—traits which Socialists hoped would become fundamental to the way of life in a new society. Thomas, however, never shared the confidence in the cooperative movement which many of his fellow Socialists held; and one of the best explanations of his skepticism appeared in a letter in the October, 1932, issue of *Cooperation:*

> I believe that the proper formation of consumers' cooperatives is ranked with the formation of a working class political party and the formation of unions as one of the fundamental forms of organization necessary in the United States. Unfortunately I believe that there is such a thing in history as the tragedy of being too late. I am inclined to think that already we are too late to organize in general successful consumers' cooperatives in the field of distribution in competition with chain stores. We shall therefore be forced to socialize the chain stores. This does not mean that I do not think consumers' cooperatives can be formed for retail distribution in connection with cooperative housing or under other favorable conditions.[24]

Although he supported the principles of the cooperation movement, his realistic assessment of the American economy had convinced him that Socialist attempts to compete with retail stores would dissipate limited Socialist organizational energies without any tangible results. Here again, his knowledge of the American scene overwhelmed traditional Socialist theory in his thought. The frankness of Thomas' assessment of the weaknesses of organized labor and the cooperative movement underscores both his awareness of the problems confronting Socialists and his faith that the proper application of Socialist principles could overcome them.

The most crucial aspect of Socialist organization, according to Thomas, was the creation of a mass-action political party. All his discussions about the nature of this party were marked by his insistence that it be, in contrast to the Republican and Democratic parties, ideologically consistent.[25] As is apparent from Thomas' writings on politics, the lack of ideological consistency disturbed him more than any other aspect of American politics. While others regarded such inconsistency as the source of the flexibility of the two-party system, Thomas saw it as the cause of irresponsible, undemocratic behavior. His preference for the party responsibility that characterizes European politics is apparent here.

The failure of the Progressive-Socialist-Radical coalition in the La Follette presidential candidacy of 1924 taught Thomas a bitter lesson: that the Socialists should continue to build their own independent organization and power in expectancy of the day that they could either become the spearhead of a new farmer-labor mass-action party or turn the Socialist party into such a movement.[26] One of the best explanations for his belief appeared in an essay in *The World Tomorrow* in 1934:

> It is clear beyond any doubt that our immediate task is to build our own organization. . . . A strong Socialist Party will be in a better position to choose its next step than a weak one. If we are to be the spearhead of a farmer-labor party, it is important that we should be as large and strong a spearhead as possible. . . . If, on the other hand, that movement outside the existing Socialist Party does not arise, if it is something for which a handful of intellectuals and others continue to agitate without great success, the more reason for us to push forward.[27]

It was essential, to Thomas, that the Socialist party continue to grow. This need explains his sympathy for the more flexible, experimental, and expansive "Militant" position in the controversy which struck the Socialist party in the 1930's.[28] Contrary to a number of scholars who charge that Thomas neglected matters of party organization, his writing reflects his preoccupation with it.[29] The failure of Socialism to achieve the powerful organization necessary to implement Thomas' goals was the result of situations beyond his control, but not, as his later writing indicates, necessarily beyond his comprehension.

II *The Cooperative Commonwealth*

As for the kind of Socialist society Thomas hoped to create, he always characterized it by using the old American radical expression, "the cooperative commonwealth." In various articles he viewed it as a society based on fellowship and cooperation—one which was practical, one which was experimental, one in which all useful groups would be represented, and one in which there need not be absolute agreement among those building Socialism.[30] However, one of the best descriptions of Thomas' concept of this society appeared in an appropriately titled article, "The World As I Want It," in the October, 1934, issue of *Forum.*

In it, Thomas noted that he had ". . .never been able to make an altogether satisfactory map of my own Utopia nor have I found any description of it which seemed to me wholly delectable."[31] He did, however, describe in general terms what he hoped would be the essential characteristics of such a society. "I want a fellowship of free men who have learned the secret of the shared abundance which the modern machine makes possible. I want a world rid once and for all of poverty, economic insecurity, and the menace of war. Such a world would release unbelievable energies for the discovery of truth and the creation of beauty."[32]

From this statement, it is easily seen that Thomas identified the cooperative commonwealth with the fullest development of human potential. This statement expressed much more than idealism; it was an expression of his faith in the potential of Socialism. However, the details of such a society would be worked out by experimentation and by the application of human reason after Socialism had been established. Thus, he concluded: "You will see that my mind dwells more on the road to power than upon a precise description of the new world."[33] The challenges in that area, as Thomas correctly surmised, proved crucial. He was too busy building Socialism to construct Utopia; therefore, his writing reflects his priorities.

III *Building Socialism: A Summation*

In 1943, *The American Mercury* published an article by Norman Thomas entitled the "Credo of an Old-Fashioned Socialist" which aptly summarized the state of his thought as he neared the end of his third decade as a Socialist. This article, while tempered by his awareness of the problems confronting Socialism, reflected both his pride and confidence in his Socialist faith. Thomas began by noting that he was an "old-fashioned socialist," the ". . .heir and beneficiary of socialist thinking and socialist traditions antedating Karl Marx."[34] Especially important to Thomas was the fact that he shared with earlier Socialist thinkers ". . .their faith that the well-being of mankind depends upon achieving a federation of co-operative commonwealths."[35]

Thomas reminded his readers that the achievement of this ideal was not automatically guaranteed because private capitalism was doomed by its own internal contradictions.[36] He was convinced that the assumption of an automatic replacement of capitalism with Socialism was the greatest error which all types of Socialists had made because it blinded them to the immensity of the task before them and especially to the role which human choice would play in the process. Thomas' warnings about Socialist overconfidence were a constant in his writings.

After asserting these general convictions, Thomas proceeded to outline what he considered to be his three basic beliefs. First, was his insistence that ". . .the fundamental problem of our time, as of other times of revolutionary change, is economic. It concerns the proper management of the resources, the physical power and the machinery which modern technology makes available to us. . . . To say that the economic problem is fundamental in this world revolution does not compel one to accept in the philosophical sense a rigorous and exclusive economic determinism."[37] The "economic problem"—Thomas' way of defining man's concern for economic security—occupied a central place in his discussion of Socialism.

The second belief which he presented was that "It is clear that the great struggle is not between economic individualism and a high degree of collectivism. It concerns the kind and amount of collectivism, and above all, whether that collectivism can be made democratic and consistent with liberty or whether it must be totalitarian."[38] Convinced that the process of combining collectivism and freedom would require a great deal of human creativity, his intense concern for civil liberties assured his continued preoccupation with this problem.

Thomas' third belief was the rejection of both the traditional Socialist definition of and faith in the infallibility of the working class: "Although the workers actively, or at least passively, will shape the future rather than the owning class, they are in no sense infallible for their own or the world's salvation. Indeed, there is no Messianic class or group. . . . The term 'worker'. . .must include all those who, by their labor of hand and brain, are adding to the common wealth."[39] Again, Thomas attempted to break what he regarded as the "dangerous" and "sterile" faith of many Socialists in the messianic working class; for he was convinced that such a misguided faith was dangerously unrealistic. Similarly, his broad definition of the term "worker" illustrates the inclusive rather than the exclusive nature of his Socialism, as well as his hope that it be a movement with popular support in all segments of the population.

The assumptions which he expressed in the 1943 article in *The American Mercury* were those which governed his writing on Socialism in the time between two world wars. The conclusion of the article, written in the depths of World War II, is convincing testimony to his belief that Socialism was the hope of mankind: "I am proud to be the heir of that tradition. I want to learn from its successes and its failures. I rejoice that I live in a day when the physical sciences have made objectively so easy the conquest of poverty. . . . The supreme insistence of democratic socialism is that plenty and freedom, peace and security are compatible in a comradeship which will cross the line of races, nationality and creed."[40] Norman Thomas had discovered and applied the proper vehicle for the realization of his humanistic reform philosophy. He was secure in his faith.

IV *Post–World War II Socialism: A Sober Reassessment*

Norman Thomas' later writings on Socialism contain a major change in emphasis which was not caused by a loss of faith in the worth of his major reform goal, the creation of a cooperative commonwealth; it was a change in tactics caused by his realistic assessment of the status of Socialism in American life. His awareness of the impact of the welfare state created by the New Deal, his increased skepticism about the efficacy of the powerful state as a tool of reform because of his observation of totalitarian states, his realization that American capitalism was not in its death throes, and his recognition of a declining Socialist electoral appeal combined to create in Thomas a far less optimistic attitude regarding the chances for short-term Socialist success in America in the post–World War II period. This loss of confidence manifested itself in his writing in a continuing discussion of the causes of Socialist failure and later in his insistence upon the need for new tactics.

Norman Thomas' discussion of the causes of the failure of Socialism in America was forthright; he presented it without recrimination or apology. His central thesis was that the failure of Socialism was the result of a combination of unique American conditions which had been exacerbated by erronous Socialist assumptions about the nature of American society. Although he alluded to the causes of Socialist failure in his 1951 volume, *A Socialist's Faith,* and in many of his post-World War II journal articles, the most comprehensive discussion of the general American conditions contributing to the weaknesses of Socialism appeared in *Socialism Re-examined* in 1963.[41]

A major part of Thomas' explanation centered on the open, mobile nature of American society. As the result of this condition, American society had less class feeling than Europe. This social mobility created a situation in which ambitious men could escape their class rather than fight for it. This possibility, in turn, created a situation, he explained, in which the potential leaders and worker solidarity which marked the rise to power of Socialism in Europe never developed in America.[42] Another important factor which Thomas felt worked against Socialist success was the nature of the American political system. The strongly entrenched two-party system, the state electoral laws, and the electoral college all limited Socialist chances for political success.[43] He placed special emphasis on the detrimental effects of the nonideological nature of American politics on Socialist attempts to establish a politically responsible, ideologically consistent party.

Another important inhibiting factor which he once more emphasized was the impact of the New Deal. Its timing was such that it preempted the formation of a genuine radical, mass-action political party in the United States. As noted before, Thomas maintained that the New Deal had averted popular destruction of capitalist institutions by preserving them in modified form through immediate reforms.[44] Thomas was convinced that the American people had been betrayed by the illusion of reform; and, in the process, Socialism had been dealt a staggering blow.

The combined impact of these three factors provided the basis for Thomas' conclusion that the failure of Socialism was to a large degree the product of events beyond the control of Socialists. He did, however, indicate in numerous instances in his later writing a number of Socialist errors which he was convinced contributed greatly to the predicament in which they found themselves. Writing in *The Virginia Quarterly Review* in the winter of 1958, Thomas discussed in detail what he regarded as the two major wrong assumptions which American Socialists had made: the notions that capitalism would die of its own contradictions and that Socialism guaranteed Utopia, concepts which, he felt, had led to a series of four additional mistakes:

> First, that man was essentially good,. . .that the proper economic system would of itself produce all needed social virtues. . . . A second assumption was that capitalism could not be sufficiently reformed to give the workers positive and enduring satisfactions. . . . Third was the assumption that once capitalism had perished and "the workers" achieved power, a socialist society would rather easily—almost automatically—solve men's problems in an atmosphere of such fellowship that the coercive state would progressively wither away. . . . Finally socialists rather blithely assumed. . .that all the problems of nationalism, colonialism, imperialism. . .would be solved because the workers of the world were uniting.[45]

From these remarks it is evident that a major crisis had developed in the later 1950's in Thomas' thinking. In the same *Virginia Quarterly Review* article, Thomas said: "On the way to advance this democratic socialism in America at this juncture in our history I am frankly puzzled."[46] Convinced that the traditional tactics were no longer relevant, Thomas developed new tactics.[47] The most detailed exposition of his new program appeared in his 1963 volume, *Socialism Re-examined.* In it, he emphasized that

"The answer to the special problems of our times for socialism does not lie in a more extensive Marxist exegesis."[48] He insisted that the program be constructed with careful regard to American realities. As he put it: "Events must guide our program and tactics."[49] Thomas noted his long struggle in the 1950's to convince the Socialist party that its limited resources of money and manpower could better be used for educational purposes rather than in presidential campaigns doomed to certain defeat. After confessing nostalgia for the old-style campaigns, Thomas argued: "It is necessary, however, to change the pattern; to show how a socialist party, under present conditions, can introduce principle and program into political discussion without depleting its limited strength, and without alienating sympathizers by running candidates who would, inevitably, merely draw away votes from the better of the two major party candidates."[50] Thomas was convinced, as has been noted earlier, that the Socialist party would be most effective if it reconstituted itself as an educational organization similar to the Fabian Society of Great Britain.[51]

Thomas emphasized that his new Socialist tactics were based on man's capacity for rationality and cooperation with his fellows.[52] The new realities which he confronted did not destroy his dream of the eventual creation of an American cooperative commonwealth. It did, however, convince him that the struggle would be more difficult than he had originally assumed. As his following remarks from the conclusion of *Socialism Re-examined* indicate, his idealism in his later career was far more restrained, far more reflective of his awareness of the complexities of human behavior than earlier in his career:

> I have been rereading Bellamy's *Looking Backward,* by which I was once deeply impressed. Now I know that men could live in his Utopia with far less happiness than he imagines would follow from its admirably just economy. . . . I crave a map of Utopia in my atlas which I cannot draw to my own satisfaction. But I do know that Utopia is not a republic of fraternity to be taken by violence. Neither can it be taken by men who have no vision of better things for mankind. In any foreseeable future, we shall be troubled with the problem of the one in relation to the many, of necessary organization and of the true freedom of the individual. Along with this problem will be the problem of bigness.[53]

Norman Thomas' later writing, which bears witness to the sobering impact of his later reassessment of declining Socialist chances in America on his reform personality, suggests that he bore the results of that reassessment with courage and dignity.

CHAPTER 5

In Defense of Civil Liberties

THE second of the major themes in Thomas' writing was his civil libertarianism. His activities on behalf of civil liberties certainly justify his reputation as one of the leading American civil libertarians of the twentieth century. Thomas initiated his advocacy of civil liberties with his impassioned defense of the rights of conscientious objectors during World War I and continued it throughout his public life. His numerous books, articles, and letters are replete with pleas for the fullest possible exercise of civil rights.

Aside from his writings and his speeches, Thomas' lifelong defense of civil liberties also involved him personally in battles against attempts to repress them. Indeed, most of his writing about them was part of his response to such controversies; and he articulated, in the face of these challenges, a remarkably consistent, coherent set of principles. Like his Socialism, his civil libertarianism was the product of a combination of strongly held philosophic convictions with the experience gained in his activities on behalf of civil rights. An examination of his writings on civil liberties provides insight, therefore, into the process whereby theory and experience merged to form a crucial part of his reform personality.

I *World War I: The Defense of Freedom of Conscience*

The first basic civil right which Thomas defended in his writing was freedom of conscience. The entry of the United States into World War I brought the young Christian pacifist face to face with the problem of conscientious objection. The war raised a basic question for Thomas and his fellow pacifists of whether or not the state could enforce its will upon a man when state demands violated the dictates of the individual's conscience. Thomas' negative answer to the question was foreordained. His own pacifism had led him at the outbreak of World War I in 1914 to join the American branch of the Fellowship of Reconciliation, a Christian pacifist group dedicated to resolving human conflict through the application of nonviolence to men's lives.[1] The American entry into the war reinforced his determination to work for the application of the principles of that group.

Thomas first stated his defense of freedom of conscience in a letter published in *The New Republic* in May, 1917.[2] The letter contained Thomas' signature at the top of a list of thirteen pacifist-objectors who called for tolerance of conscientious objectors. Both the style and the nature of the arguments presented indicate that Thomas wrote it. The letter begins with a justification of conscientious objection on the grounds of human diversity. Asserting that "In the evolution of the human mind we discover a gradually widening hiatus between physical competence and intellectual moral competence," Thomas noted that some men were best suited to physical courage, others to "intelligent" acts of courage, and still others to "moral bravery." He maintained that such varieties of human temperament provided a logical basis for tolerance of different kinds of human behavior.[3] In this way, Thomas laid the groundwork for his justification of conscientious objection as one of the diverse forms of human behavior deserving such tolerance.

Thomas went straight to the point: ". . .there is a type of man to whom (military) participation in war is tantamount to committing murder. He cannot, he will not, commit murder. There is no human power on God's earth that can coerce him into committing (what *he* knows to be) the act of murder. . . . Shall he be maltreated for his scruples? Or shall he be respected (as his deriders are) for his conscientiousness?[4] Unswayed by the patriotic fever which was sweeping the country, he proceeded to fully develop arguments for tolerance of conscientious objection on several grounds.

Thomas' initial argument for tolerance of conscientious objection was based on the proven importance of dissent in time of peace.[5] If such tolerance was important in peacetime, Thomas reasoned, it was even more critical in wartime when there was even more danger resulting from the temptation of the government to crush tolerance of diversity and differing opinions in pursuit of national security. Tolerance of the conscientious objector would be one important indication that the precious freedom of dissent had not been destroyed in wartime. It is apparent from his remarks in this letter that he felt that the immediate rights of the small minority of men involved was part of a far broader problem. It was not that their freedom of conscience was unimportant but that their right to dissent as individuals went to the heart of the American way of life. The suppression of that right would empty other civil liberties of their meaning.

A second and even more compelling argument for the defense of conscientious objection, according to Thomas, grew from the need for the reconstruction which would inevitably follow the war. As he explained, ". . .sooner or later war must cease. The tremendous enterprise of recreating out of bloody chaos some new, reinspired internationalism will be the order of the day. Who is better fitted for that reconstructive task than those humanists now in imminent danger of being bullied out of existence because their visions and their faiths extend beyond the time of bloody chaos?"[6] Thomas was convinced that the vanguard of the post-war civilization would be composed of those whose minds looked beyond war as an instrument of human decision making to the development of a peaceful world. It was, therefore, essential that they be permitted to live in freedom until their time would come. The conscientious objector was an important link, a bridge between the harsh realities of the present and the hopes of the future.

In yet another argument, Thomas and his co-signers maintained that it would be tragic if the United States extinguished freedom at home while in the process of carrying it to the rest of the world. Again, the point was posed in the form of a question: "In bringing the gift of freedom to the distant unemancipated shall we betray so precious a cause by brute denial of freedom to those of our own blood and tradition, to our own freedom-lovers within the gate?"[7] To prevent such a situation, Thomas urged that President Woodrow Wilson appoint men and women to the draft Exemption Boards who were "conspicuous for their social service"—settlement workers, publicists, and educators. He was convinced that such persons, imbued as they were with the concept of service to mankind, would be more tolerant of the beliefs of conscientious objectors. Individual conscience and societal good merged in the arguments presented by Thomas in favor of conscientious objection. So also did his idealism and practicality.

Like his other World War I experiences, Norman Thomas' defense of conscientious objection proved to be one of the major influences which shaped his reform personality. The threat to freedom of conscience that he saw in the coercion of individual objectors reinforced his belief in the need for the continued protection of dissent in American society. This belief, combined with his devout pacifism, motivated Thomas to write his book, *The Conscientious Objector in America,* which was first published in 1923.[8] He repeated the point developed in his wartime letters that there were many kinds of bravery and that conscientious objection was equally as courageous as battlefield valor.[9]

Asserting that there were two major problems confronting his generation, ". . .the relation of the individual to the state" and ". . .how to end war before war ends civilization," Thomas described how the treatment of conscientious objectors during World War I was related to both. He acknowledged his intention to state the facts fairly but not to avoid his own point of view which was premised on the assumption that the ". . .state has. . .no right to conscript men's lives for service wholly opposed to their own convictions."[10] He pointed out that he was writing the volume at the behest of the National Civil Liberties Bureau, the forerunner of the modern American Civil Liberties Union, because of the desire of that organization to record some of the aspects of the first national experience with conscription in American society because of its possible significance for future generations.[11]

Thomas proceeded to write a graphic account of the experiences of conscientious objectors during the war which surveyed the varieties of conscientious objection, the nature of the government's policies toward the objectors, and their impact on individual objectors. These aspects make Thomas' the most comprehensive study of conscientious objection during World War I. In it, he developed what was to be his standard approach in later works—a synthesis based on a combination of the research of others and his own experiences. The result was a strongly argued condemnation of the way objectors, including his brother Evan, were misunderstood and mistreated by their fellow Americans. The major arguments which he presented were all amplifications of those originally presented in his defense of conscientious objection in his wartime letters. *Is Conscience a Crime?* illustrates how his beliefs in freedom of conscience and pacifism reinforced each other and shaped his reform personality.

Thomas placed the blame for the suppression of freedom of conscience on the Wilson administration, the church, and liberals. However, he did not ignore the emotions and irrationality generated by the war that contributed to the situation in America. As he described it, "Individuals were more or less pawns in the hands of the mighty passions they had unloosed to goad the people into war."[12] His cognizance of the powerful impact of the emotional atmosphere in the country gave him another justification for condemning the results of war.

Criticism of the government's refusal to honor the absolutist conscientious objector's unwillingness to subordinate his conscience to the will of the state was an important part of Thomas' indictment. He was sure that ". . .all philosophic defenses of conscription are government rationales of the fear that without conscription the protection of that sacred entity of the nation, might be impossible."[13] Conscientious objection was an effective antidote against the doctrine of the divinity of the state which threatened to subordinate all expressions of freedom to its desires. As he observed, "Men's affairs are in sorry plight if it serves society to compel the individual to be true to his fellows by being untrue to himself."[14] The experience of the objectors were proof to Thomas that it was time for some fresh thinking on the duty of civil disobedience, and he urged his readers to remember the beliefs of Henry David Thoreau because he felt they would cause increased respect for the objector's refusal to act against the dictates of his conscience.[15]

Another important aspect of Thomas' criticism centered on the reaction of the Christian Church to conscientious objection. His disillusionment with the church regarding its attitude toward conscientious objectors was apparent throughout the volume.[16] Thomas' earlier criticism of the church in 1917, and his criticism of it in *Is Conscience a Crime?* and in subsequent writings make it clear that he never forgave the Christian Church for its refusal to support freedom of conscience for individual objectors. It was certainly one of if not the principal cause of his rejection of the church in favor of Socialism.[17]

Thomas believed that the issue of conscientious objection raised a crucial question for the church about the compatibility of war and Christianity. He noted that many of the objectors based their faith on the New Testament and insisted that they were maintaining a higher loyalty to God that transcended the necessity of "rendering unto Caesar what was Caesar's." He was certain that ". . .a careful reading of the New Testament certainly suggests that the burden of proof rests heavily upon those who would reconcile Christianity and war."[18] The influence of the Fellowship of Reconciliation on Thomas was evident in his condemnation of the Christian Church's support of the war effort. In assessing the impact of that organization, Thomas said: "Some of them, like the author of the book, probably owed to the Fellowship much of the impulse which opened their eyes to the incompatibility of war and Christianity."[19] Thomas' justification of freedom of conscience was inseparably linked to his Christian pacifism.

Thus, while the state committed grievous wrongs against the objectors, Thomas felt that the failure of the church to speak even on behalf of mercy for the imprisoned objector was worse because of its Christian tradition.[20] Thomas added that he had less difficulty talking with the military officials and the War Department about the treatment of objectors than he had with officials of the church. He added a typically ironic comment that many Protestant churchmen refused to accept the right of absolutist objectors to exercise their freedom of conscience and refuse military service while accepting without protest their own exemption from military service because they were ministers.[21] To Thomas, the conclusion was inescapable: "If the state did not prove itself the exemplar of what many had thought were American traditions of liberty and conscience, the Christian Church did worse. What the Churches gave us was a thoroughgoing religion of the state."[22] The failure of the church to defend the tradition of freedom of conscience, an important part ot its own tradition, bitterly disappointed Thomas.

The last group which drew Thomas' critical fire for not coming to the aid of the objectors was the liberals. While he realized that the war fever and the post-war Red Scare both created conditions conducive to the nonsupport of civil liberties, he nevertheless insisted that circumstances ". . .do not in equal degree help us to forgive the almost total failure of a stalwart minority of liberals to function in this crisis."[23] The freedom of conscience which Thomas felt was at stake in the treatment of the objectors was too important a value to surrender even under pressure. *Is Conscience a Crime?* is a statement of Thomas' dismay because the important groups which he criticized did not realize that the principle at stake in the conscientious-objector controversy was such a crucial one for the future of the country. The volume reiterates the high position of freedom of conscience in his scale of values. Written after his conversion to Socialism, it stands as proof that his conversion did not lessen his concern for freedom of conscience.

II *The Pursuit of Justice in the 1920's: The Mooney-Billings Case*

Thomas' stout defense of freedom of conscience was only one manifestation of his highly developed sense of fair play, for justice in all aspects of American life. Especially disturbing to Thomas in the 1920's was the willingness of many Americans to condone the misuse of the legal system to deny the liberties of those who criticized American society and dissented from the prevalent beliefs of the majority. This sensitivity to the miscarriage of justice was clearly illustrated by Thomas' writings on behalf of Thomas J. Mooney and Warren K. Billings, the convicted labor radicals.

Both men had been convicted and sentenced to long prison terms for alleged involvement in a bombing which took place during the 1916 Preparedness Day parade in San Francisco.[24] Public feeling against radicalism had run so strong during their trial that, even though both men insisted that they were nowhere near the scene of the disturbance, the testimony of witnesses who later admitted that they had perjured themselves led to their conviction and to long prison sentences. Anti-radical feelings, fear of political reprisals, and Mooney's stubborn refusal to petition for parole kept the men in prison long after their innocence was no longer in doubt.

Thomas, convinced that the men were innocent, became one of the leading advocates of their release. One of his best pleas for Mooney's release appeared in the October 24, 1928, issue of *The Nation.*[25] In it, Thomas used a visit with Mooney in San Quentin Prison to create reader sympathy by portraying Mooney as a human being who had suffered greatly because of a horrible miscarriage of justice.[26] Thomas vehemently denied rumors circulating in labor circles that Mooney was bitter, intractable, and unreasonable because of his refusal to accept a parole. He interpreted Mooney's insistence on his total innocence as a sign of courage.[27]

He continued by contrasting the Mooney-Billings case favorably with other cases involving the persecution of radicals. He argued that there was, for example, a clear-cut difference between it and the Sacco-Vanzetti case where those who wished ". . .can clutch the poor rags of belief, real or pretended, in the guilt of the two Italians."[28] There was, on the other hand, no doubt regarding the innocence of Mooney and Billings. "But in the guilt of Mooney and Billings for the bomb outrage on San Francisco's Preparedness Day no intelligent man believes. Their colleagues were all acquitted, the perjured evidence against them has long since been confessed. The jury and the prosecuting attorney have joined in petitioning for their pardon. Judge Franklin A. Griffin, who sentenced them, is one of the most earnest workers for their vindication."[29] Thomas then expressed pessimism about the chances for a full pardon because of political and economic pressures on the governor of California.[30]

The principle at issue in the Mooney-Billings case was a crucial one to Thomas. It, like his defense of freedom of conscience, was based on his belief that it had lasting significance for those interested in the preservation of American liberties. As he put it: "Mooney can stand prison better than we can stand having him there. A country which after the Sacco-Vanzetti case keeps Mooney and Billings in jail is a country without elemental knowledge of what justice means."[31] He was convinced that miscarriages of justice such as he saw in the Mooney-Billings case would destroy the faith of Americans in our legal system.

Thomas concluded by noting that the same waters which washed the walls of San Quentin Prison also washed the shores of President Herbert Hoover's home at Palo Alto. He did so to show that the moral responsibility for injustice extended to the very top of American society. As Thomas asserted, "We have a right to know how a President would react to this human problem and to take his measure if he is as silent and as acquiescent in this monstrous crime against American freedom as he was in the oil scandals."[32] *The Nation* article exemplifies both the intensity of Thomas' belief in justice and the nature of his persuasive writing.

III *Some Thoughts on the Nature of Liberty*

One of the fullest expositions of Thomas' concept of the nature of liberty appeared in his review essay of Everett Dean Martin's book, *Liberty,* in the June 7, 1930, issue of *The Saturday Review of Literature.*[33] Relying on experience rather than on absolute principles as the basis of his definition and his justification of liberty, Thomas described it in terms of the good which it had brought mankind:[34] "It has been proved that heresy is the growing point of society and the successful suppression of heresy is not merely a blow to liberty but the beginning of social stagnation. This is again to justify liberty in terms of the discovery of truth and individual freedom in terms of social well-being—a humbler but sounder argument than high talk of absolute rights."[35] The pragmatism inherent in Thomas' civil libertarianism is very much in evidence in the essay in his view that liberty is an essential cause of human progress.

Thomas also saw another "humble but persuasive" argument in favor of the protection of civil liberties in modern times. It was centered on the idea that ". . .a machine age necessarily requires such a degree of cooperation and even standardization over wide areas of human life that it becomes more important than ever before to stress freedom for the individual in all these matters where it is not very clearly opposed to the good of society."[36] The defense of civil liberties would also serve as the guardian of human values in the face of advancing technology.

In concluding his review of the Martin book, Thomas noted that the author in stating that liberty would ". . .not be won by the crowd by any sort of mass action. . ." had done two things against which his readers should beware.[37] He first charged that Martin had ". . .minimized and almost ignored the economic roots of the grossest denials of freedom in America."[38] Admitting that the "crowd" had played active parts in the Sacco-Vanzetti and Mooney-Billings cases, Thomas insisted that the original acts of wrong in these and many other miscarriages of justice began with men ". . .who for the sake of economic profits and power have not only sinned against every concept of liberty but betrayed the most elemental notions of justice."[39] Here again, the influences of Thomas' work among the poor of New York City during his urban ministry and his observations of life among the exploited during the 1920's and the Depression years shaped his thinking.

Thomas' second criticism of the Martin book centered on its failure to consider the functions of government. Again eschewing theory, Thomas emphasized that the problem was one of making government ". . .a useful servant rather than an absolute master."[40] The growth of governmental functions must, he insisted, be accompanied by increased public interest and control. In this way, he reiterated his belief in the fundamental union of democratic control and human freedom. As he said, "For he who would save democracy must increase the love of liberty and the capacity for liberty. Likewise he who would save liberty must put his trust in democracy."[41] Only the preservation of the peace upon which all other aspects of human progress depended proved more fundamental in the thinking of Norman Thomas.

IV *The 1930's and 1940's: The Fear of Domestic Totalitarianism*

It is not surprising in light of Thomas' beliefs in the necessity of the active exercise of civil liberties that his writing in the 1930's and 1940's reflected his increasing concern over what he felt were growing threats to human liberty in the United States. As has been noted before, the growth of Depression-reinforced totalitarianism abroad made him more acutely aware of the necessity of preserving American liberties. What follows is an analysis of Thomas' writings in defense of civil liberties in three different areas of American life which illustrates the breadth and intensity of his concern for human freedom.

The first area to be considered is Thomas' defense of

academic freedom. In June, 1931, an outstanding professor, Herbert Adolphus Miller, was fired from Ohio State University because of his call for optional rather than compulsory military training at that institution. After a careful investigation of the events leading to Professor Miller's dismissal, Thomas published an article in the June 17, 1931, issue of *The Nation* which discussed its significance.[42] In it, he maintained that the firing was important because "Not for many years has there been so clear a demonstration that a Board of trustees, dominated by the usual business ideals, expects its students to be docile Babbits in embryo, its university president to be a high-grade office manager, and its faculty to conform or get out."[43] Thomas' analysis of the events in the Ohio State situation made it clear that his criticism was based on a much deeper concern than his traditional Socialist antipathy to business influence.

Such a situation, he felt, created a threefold threat to American liberty. The first could be seen in the challenge which the case presented to American youth. Those students going to Ohio State ". . .will know that he and his professors on certain vital matters must think—or at any rate talk—as [Chief Trustee,] Mr. Julius Stone thinks proper or get out."[44] To Thomas, such an education was antithetical to the tolerance of diversity, the ideal of humanitarian service, and the democratic values which he regarded as the basis of progress.

The second danger was one which, he felt, concerned the entire academic profession: "Acquiescence in the Ohio situation is unadorned prostitution of loyalty to truth, to be excused only for the same economic reasons that excuse the women who follow the oldest of professions."[45] He was certain that college teaching without academic freedom was ". . .an intellectual slavery worse than the devotion of any theologian to a rigid creed."[46] So great was his desire to defend academic freedom that he urged professors to blacklist universities which violated it.

Even more important, insisted Thomas, was the fact that the situation at Ohio State raised the ". . .question of the competence of democracy and the validity of its ideals."[47] Observing that the American state university was the product of democracy's hunger for education, he concluded "That is not education which subordinates the quest for truth to the service of existing prejudice. Democracy fastens on itself its own chains whenever in the name of patriotism or any popular prejudice it lets its own friends and servants, the seekers after truth, be made the victims of that sort of disguised economic dictatorship."[48] He justified academic freedom on the grounds that its existence was one of the proofs that liberty continued to exist. Both the continued existence of freedom of inquiry and its pragmatic implications were essential parts of Thomas' concept of freedom.

Thomas broadened his discussion of academic freedom to include the secondary and elementary schools in subsequent writings during the 1930's, and his arguments underscored again the pragmatic basis of his libertarian beliefs. One such example appeared in the May, 1932, issue of *Progressive Education* in which he advocated the need for schools to discuss controversial matter "frankly and fairly."[49] He began by asserting that public education had failed to live up to the expectations of those who hoped that it would strengthen democracy because it had turned out standardized products who had been ". . .taught to read but not to think."[50] But even worse than standardization was the conformity which Thomas saw as its by-product: "The educational machine is beautiful and fairly expensive. We pour our children into the hopper, and the machine grinds out an assorted lot of Babbitts and Robots with their appropriate prejudices."[51] Such conformity excluded the creative social thought necessary for the meaningful application of democratic values. This effect, Thomas argued, was especially dangerous because it was occurring at a time when it prevented the necessary understanding and control of the immense increase in man's knowledge of technology. He charged the schools with perpetuating a serious form of cultural lag. His argument has been restated recently by Alvin Toffler in his widely-discussed book, *Future Shock.*

To counteract this situation, Thomas proposed a four-point plan to make education more realistic:

1. We must recognize that controversial issues cannot be avoided, and that to teach children and young people to face them fairly and intelligently is the main business of education. . . .

2. We must fairly present the facts and then offer a fair statement of the contending interpretations of those facts. . . .

3. Such education is only possible when we select teachers. . .and then give them freedom both as teachers and citizens to serve the great cause of truth. . . .

4. Finally, if we are to train our children to face controversial issues, we must let them have some experience in being citizens and not merely subjects in the schools.[52]

It was important to Thomas that truth emerge from the honest conflict of ideas in the intellectual marketplace. An education based on freedom of inquiry and the confrontation of controversial issues would prepare the students realistically for the complex, varied alternatives which they would confront as citizens of a democratic society.

Another major concern of Thomas' in the 1930's was the suppression of civil liberties which he felt was the result of the growth of domestic Fascism in American society. His personal involvement in defense of freedom of assembly and of the right to picket in an Indiana labor dispute in 1935 provides an example of how Thomas' own experience reinforced his conviction that the danger from domestic Fascism was great, and it also illustrates how his own experience added realism to his reform writings. Thomas summarized what he regarded as the significance of his experience in Indiana in an article, "Hoosier Hitlerism," in the September 18, 1935, issue of *The Nation.*[53] Written in the midst of a legal battle in which Thomas and other Socialists were trying to force the removal of martial law from strike-torn Sullivan and Vigo counties in Indiana, the article illustrates the intensity of his hatred of Fascism and the dangers that he saw in its domestic manifestations.

Thomas began by noting that the citizens of the two Indiana counties were denied their liberties because Governor McNutt had declared martial law. Particularly appalling to Thomas was the nature of the martial law and the reasons for its application. The Indiana authorities had developed a ". . .new instrument for the economical and effective denial of civil liberties. . ." by substituting enforcement of martial law by civil rather than by military authorities in the two counties.[54] Thomas insisted that such an application was contrary to the plain intent of the Indiana constitution which forbade the subordination of civil to military authorities.[55] He regarded the Indiana situation as a dangerous precedent, one whose danger became apparent when one viewed the results and the intent of those who established martial law. The law, he felt, enabled the "...authorities to help their friends of the Chamber of Commerce and the Manufacturers' Association to circumvent the rather liberal civil laws of Indiana, which give to labor the right of peaceful picketing and curb the use of the injunction against labor."[56] The martial law as applied in the two counties operated as an effective strikebreaking weapon by subverting the normal legal guarantees against such actions. Thomas felt that the action was premised on the same disdain of the civil rights of individuals which had marked the triumph of Fascism in Europe.

Thomas escaped the charge that he was merely letting his sympathy for organized labor blind him to the fact that the martial law in Sullivan and Vigo counties was necessitated by labor violence by presenting a convincing discussion of the broader implications of the events in Indiana. Emphasizing that "...one or two legal points are important," he pointed out how "The Indiana constitution expressly subordinates military to civil law. The Governor in his proclamation did the exact opposite. . . . The whole justification of martial law is the existence of a situation in which the civil police cannot function effectively. When martial law prevails in counties where no troops are needed to enforce it, its ostensible justification has obviously disappeared."[57] The danger, Thomas thought, lay in the precedent which the particular form of martial law set: "But if the forerunners of fascism in America find that Governor McNutt can get away with this sort of thing its use will spread like wildfire. Hitler never thought of anything better. Acquiescence in it is acquiescence in tyranny."[58] Thomas saw a very real connection between local practices which denied civil liberty and the growth of Fascism in America. Because of this, he urged those who were opposed to Fascism to condemn Indiana's use of martial law. Thomas was convinced that the active defense of civil liberties was the best means of defending American society from the growth of the totalitarian spirit. Certain as he was in the 1930's that the struggle was one in which the alternatives were a totalitarian state or a cooperative commonwealth, the struggle seemed eminently worthwhile. Here, as in other aspects of Thomas' thought, the connection between the theoretical and the real was so intimate that it was impossible to distinguish between them.

The preservation of domestic civil liberties continued to be one of Thomas' major concerns during World War II. His writing in that period indicates that his more recently developed fear of domestic Fascism was reinforced by his painful memories of the repression of civil liberties in the name of patriotism which had occurred during World War I. Perhaps the best example of the confluence of these ideas can be seen in his writings on the forced evacuation of the Japanese-Americans from the West Coast for security reasons in early 1942. His most detailed discussion of the Japanese evacuation question appeared in an article entitled "Dark Day for Liberty" in the July 29, 1942, issue of *The Christian Century.*[59] He introduced his subject by observing that civil liberties seemed less endangered in the weeks after Pearl Harbor than they had at the time of American entry into World War I. A solemn reappraisal precipitated by the removal of the Japanese, however, had convinced him that American liberty was in greater danger than it had been during World War I because "Our disease was like a rash then, conspicuous, painful and perhaps for that reason more easily curable. It is now more like a cancer, deep seated and scarcely recognized by the average citizen."[60]

Thomas justified his conclusion on two grounds: first, the President had "assumed and passed on" to the army ". . .wholly totalitarian controls over American citizens;"[61] second, for the first time in American history, men, committees, and publications boasting of their liberalism ". . .are in the vanguard of justifying the presidential assumption of dictatorial power."[62] He pointed out that patriotic fever was at such a high pitch that those who ordinarily defended civil liberties did not fully understand the implications of the Japanese evacuation policy. These facts caused Thomas to conclude ominously that civil liberties would be more difficult to defend than during World War I. The evacuation of the Japanese was proof to Thomas that the latent totalitarianism which he had observed earlier could develop quickly in a wartime atmosphere. To make his arguments more meaningful, Thomas addressed himself to the results of the evacuation of the Japanese-Americans:

Seventy thousand American citizens from the so-called First Area in from the west coast have been evacuated from their homes and businesses and schools into more or less well run concentration camps. In the process they have suffered a property loss which I have heard conservatively estimated at 60 per cent of all their holdings. Japanese-American residents in the Second Area far back from the west coast are now under serious restrictions and will soon be evacuated. Not one of these men and women has been charged with any crime or misdemeanor. No act of sabotage has even been alleged against them.[63]

Thomas then drew an ironic contrast between the treatment of these Japanese-Americans with those in Hawaii who had not been placed under any restrictions despite the sabotage discovered there. This contrast led him to conclude that "What was and is being done in the west was born of panic, race prejudice and greed for Japanese-American property. It is justified unconvincingly in the name of military necessity, and on the further ground that it is necessary to protect these citizens from mob violence."[64] He was convinced that the Japanese-Americans were the innocent victims of a horrible crime.

Especially disheartening to Thomas was his inability to "arouse" the American public about the issue. Americans, he felt, did not realize that the presidential proclamation ordering the evacuation of the Japanese-Americans could have been applied to them. He was especially critical of the American Civil Liberties Union of which he was a director for supporting the constitutionality of the presidential proclamation. He also criticized Congress for the complacency reflected in its willingness to pass legislation punishing those who disobeyed the evacuation orders.[65] Indeed, to Thomas, the acceptance of the Japanese evacuation was a manifestation of totalitarianism. "There could scarcely be a more complete acceptance of the totalitarian theory of justice, which is that the interest of the state, as interpreted by its rulers, is the highest standard of right, to which all individual interests must be subordinate."[66] The danger was in the precedent which it set. The denial of the civil rights of one group on the grounds of national security, he warned, could lead to total mobilization of Americans, to rigid censorship, and to the silencing of all those who criticized any aspect of the war effort.

Thus, Thomas' response to the Japanese evacuation question was motivated by alarm. He hoped his writing about it would ". . .arouse thoughtful Americans out of an unwarranted complacency about civil liberties, and to enlist them in organizing public opinion and putting pressure on the government to cure the cancer of totalitarianism whose beginnings are so clearly marked in the fate of Americans of Japanese descent."[67] That his fellow Americans did not view the situation as he did is indicative of the exalted place of civil liberties in his thought and of his hypersensitivity to what he felt were threats to their exercise. He refused to sacrifice his belief in their sanctity even to what the majority of his fellow citizens regarded, rightly or wrongly, as the demands of national security.

CHAPTER 6

Civil Liberties: The Later Years

I *Civil Liberties During the Cold War: The Complexity of the Communist Issue*

THE advent of the Cold War and the insecurity which it created in American society after 1945 presented new challenges for the civil libertarianism of Norman Thomas.[1] American concern with the threat of world Communism created a new, more complex version of the dilemma posed by the conflicting demands of individual freedom and national security than Thomas had previously faced. Confronted with this dilemma, Thomas struggled to find a middle ground which would preserve civil liberties in the face of those who justified their restriction for reasons of national security but, at the same time, allow for the fact that the threat of Communism was a very real one.

As stated previously, Thomas had never been a totally uncritical admirer of the Sovet Union. In the 1930's, his own travels in Russia, his contacts with the victims of Soviet tyranny, the Soviet purge trials, Stalin's rapprochement with Hitler, and the disruptive behavior of the Communist party of the United States had convinced him that Communism was as great a threat to human freedom as Fascism. His continued criticism of Soviet totalitarianism during World War II made him highly unpopular because of America's wartime alliance with Russia. In the post-war years, Thomas never allowed his hatred of Communism to lead him to the extremes to which it led many other Americans during the mass anti-Communist hysteria which swept over the country. His response was governed, on one hand, by his firmly held beliefs about the importance of freedom and, on the other, by the conviction born of experience that Communism presented a unique challenge to American democracy. Thomas' writing faithfully portrays his attempt to develop a viable philosophy of civil libertarianism in the light of this challenge. In so doing, it reveals much of the dilemma which Communism created for traditional civil libertarians such as Thomas.

Several of Thomas' essays written in the era that American hysteria over Communism was at its peak—in the late 1940's and early 1950's—are particularly valuable for the insights into Thomas' thoughts which they provide. One of the clearest expositions of his thinking appeared in the article "Civil Rights—But Not Conspiracy" published in the January 7, 1951, *The New York Times Magazine.*[2] Premising his argument on the assumption that neither hysteria nor blindness to Communist intrigue could guarantee liberty, Thomas explored the alternatives.

He began his article with a characterization of the traditional American philosophy of civil liberties and the way it had developed into a generally accepted group of rights and practices. He explained how these civil liberties rested on two major assumptions: ". . .the first, that man was something less than man unless he was possessed of the right to fair trial and to freedom of conscience, communication, assemblage and association; the second, that society itself was most secure when ideas had their chance to win or lose in the full competition of the marketplace."[3] In his discussion of the subsequent development of these principles, Thomas emphasized that, while there were occasions when men might feel it their right or duty to fight against injustice, ". . .no society or government can include the right to revolution among its civil liberties to be protected by law."[4] The use of a brief historical survey to introduce his subject was a common feature of his writing. In this essay, he used it as the basis of a contrast which was crucial to his argument.

He developed this contrast in a discussion of the impact of Communism on American civil liberties. Here, he dwelled on the uniqueness of Communists among American radical groups. He carefully pointed out that the Communist advocacy of force and violence was not the characteristic which set them apart. Calling again on history to prove his point, he noted that Emma Goldman and her fellow anarchists had advocated violence before World War I and how even Thomas

Jefferson had admitted instances where it might be useful. As Norman Thomas illustrated, the Communist threat had its origins in something far more complex than the advocacy of violence: "The new element which the Communists have injected into the picture is their assertion of a right to the protection of laws which in power they would abolish, a right to do in the American community that which they would punish by slavery or death if they should come to power."[5] He was convinced that their support of civil liberties was opportunistic and hypocritical rather than genuine as in the case of other radical groups who sought to exercise them.

With a bitterness born of experience, Thomas pointed out yet another vital but oft-repeated distinction between the Communists and other radical groups: "These Communists are the first dissenting group in American history to make a virtue of lies and deceit, the first to reduce all social ethics to the appalling simplicity of the commandment: 'Thou shall at all times obey party orders. There is no other mortal law.' "[6] Such were the reasons that formed the basis of his plea that a unique approach was necessary to the civil liberties of those who professed allegiance to the Communist party.

Thomas then supported his indictment of the Communist party by citing examples of its behavior. He noted with sarcasm that during World War II there were many staunch defenders of civil liberties who felt the Communists were not so bad as he had implied and that their tactics did not present a "clear and present danger."[7] He then described the events which had destroyed that impression for many such as the Communist coup in Czechoslovakia, the Hiss case, Communist attempts to infiltrate American labor, and their hypocritical treatment of Earl Browder, the deposed Communist party leader, after his indictment for contempt of Congress. After discussing these events, Thomas posed a question: "What should believers in the Jeffersonian doctrine of civil liberties do when confronted with these facts?"[8] He answered his own question by recalling that Jefferson had moved vigorously against the Aaron Burr conspiracy and by posing another question: "Would he have expected us to apply his faith in the power of truth in the face not of flamboyantly honest rebels of the older pattern but of a conspiratorial party?"[9] The answer which he expected was obvious: some restrictive action would have to be taken against the Communists.

The problem, then, was one of finding a standard which would realistically control the unique nature of Communist behavior. Thomas emphasized that, while he did not feel that mere membership in the Communist party should send a man to jail, it should be adequate cause to keep him out of sensitive government positions and teaching jobs. He justified this position with the argument that ". . .the guilt of surrendering one's freedom of mind and inquiry to a conspiratorial party should be enough to bar a person from a teacher's chair."[10] In this manner, he turned aside the arguments of those absolutist civil libertarians who cautioned against condemning individual Communists through guilt by association.

Thomas then discussed the problems created by the Communist concealment of their party affiliations. This conspiratorial behavior had led the United States government ". . .to use procedures in police work and investigation which, in their very nature, as all history shows, can easily be subverted to the immense hurt of the innocent and the whole concept of freedom. It is far easier to catch the innocent and honest dissenter whose expression of opinion is entitled to protection than it is to catch the conspirator."[11] In this way, he drew a cause-and-effect pattern from Communist deceit to the mood of repression which led to threats against the liberty of honest reformers and dissenters.

The last section of the essay is a general discussion of the dangers of overreacting to the Communist menace. He expressed dismay that "The contagion of repression, the zeal for enforced conformity, easily spreads in government and the mob."[12] As an example, he cited the pressure to deny broadcast and television access to the variety of opinions which others regard as Communist. He told how The National Broadcasting Corporation had received some 350 calls protesting its radio documentary which had praised the Bill of Rights. Such behavior, he feared, underscored the very real danger that Americans could lose their freedoms ". . .by imitation of the enemy for the sake of victory."[13] This danger,

Thomas felt, posed a much more immediate threat than either a military defeat or internal subversion by the Communists.

What kind of approach did Thomas feel would ". . .protect the national security, the rights of the individual, and the orderly processes of democracy at one and the same time against conspiratorial Communists and despotic police power"?[14] The primary point which he emphasized was his conviction that the problem was not a matter to be solved by relying solely on either libertarian theory or physical security. What was necessary, then, was a pragmatic approach to the problem of balancing liberty and security.[15] Having already rejected the arguments of the extreme civil libertarians earlier in the essay, Thomas turned his guns on the advocates of extreme security. He cited the McCarren Internal Security Act as one which, though constitutional and created for a commendable purpose, was "enormously hurtful" in action because it burned down the barn to get rid of the rats.[16] He attacked the domestic registration provisions of the act as unrealistic, the alien registration provisions as the cause of irritation abroad, and the general tendency of the act to paralyze honest thinking and discussion on important public questions. Formal regulations to ensure security did not impress Thomas.

Thomas concluded his *Times Magazine* essay with an admonition: "Just because we cannot settle our problems by easy appeal to any libertarian scriptures, we must be the more careful lest in the name of fighting communism or any other totalitarianism we lay its foundation in America."[17] This fear lies at the heart of Thomas' plea for a sensible response to the Cold War, for such had been the impact of Communism during the Cold War on Norman Thomas.

When the continued growth of anti-Communist hysteria in the early 1950's—one encouraged by the activities of Senator Joseph McCarthy of Wisconsin and by other professional anti-Communists—created a mood of repression in the United States that threatened civil liberties, Thomas published in 1954 *The Test of Freedom* in which he amplified the seminal ideas originally presented in his 1951 *New York Times Magazine* article. The volume is a detailed, passionate indictment of both Communist and McCarthyite tactics because of the dangers they posed for American democracy. The book illustrates his continued preoccupation with his attempt to develop a viable philosophy of civil libertarianism in the face of what he felt were the twin threats of Communist subversion and the repression which it generated. Although a detailed discussion of its contents would be needlessly repetitious because of the parallels with the previously discussed 1951 *New York Times Magazine* article, some mention of the conclusion is in order because it illustrates the way in which the Cold War had reinforced his belief in the importance of civil liberties. Certain that America had ". . .become the world's one best hope,. . ." he saw the existence of freedom as the essential element in what America symbolized to the world.[18]

This belief convinced Thomas that "It is for us to prove that neither communism nor McCarthyism is the end of the American dream."[19] The "test of freedom," then, was its ability to withstand the threats of both—to convince the world that it could withstand the threat of totalitarianism, despite its source, without sacrificing American liberties. The significance of *The Test of Freedom* is threefold: first, it is a warning to the American people lest they become like their enemies by using totalitarian methods against them; second, the volume indicates Thomas' awareness of the world-wide implications of the defense of American liberties; third, it is another expression of Thomas' faith in man's ability to overcome the problems confronting him regardless of their complexity. The work should be read, therefore, with these three aspects in mind.

II *The Defense of Dissent*

Another important aspect of Thomas' writing on civil liberties in the post–World War II era was his exposition of the importance of dissent, which was not a new topic for Thomas; for, like all of the important premises of his civil libertarianism, its roots could be traced to his experiences in World War I. However, the immense pressure for conformity generated by both the Cold War and the corporate mentality after 1945 convinced Thomas that the time was ripe for a renewed exposition of the values of dissent in a free society.[20] The result was a number of essays and the book *Great Dissenters* in which Thomas expounded his long-held beliefs in the importance of dissent.[21]

An essay, "The Dissenter's Role in a Totalitarian Age," in the November 20, 1949, issue of *The New York Times Magazine* clearly illustrates the major assumptions underlying his philosophy of dissent, the reasons he regarded it as so important, and the basic consistency of his thoughts about the subject.[22] In it, Thomas developed the thesis that the real dissenter was needed more than ever in a world threatened by totalitarianism. He opened the essay by repeating what had long been the major premise underlying his belief in dissent: that it was one of the important causes of social progress. To this basic point, he added a corollary: when dissent is repressed, society stagnates.[23] Like so many other aspects of his civil libertarianism, his faith in dissent was anchored on a combination of historical experience and pragmatism.

Thomas pointed out that the problems related to the defense of dissent were far more complex than formerly because modern conflicts were not between individual prophets and their groups but between rival groups with different "interests and ideologies." As an example, he emphasized that neither the Communists nor the Fascists deserved to be called dissenters because each was ". . .merely the docile but often fanatic slave to his own particular group and its leaders" who would tolerate ". . .no true freedom of dissent."[24] Even more disturbing was the lack of any dissent which he found in American society. He explained this situation in the following terms: "The list of dissenters even in America who have been held back in their trade or profession, or blacklisted altogether, who have faced hostile audiences or ugly mobs, who have known arrest or imprisonment is long, but it is very short compared with men who have been kept in line simply by fear of being different, or by determination to keep up with the Joneses."[25] This compulsion for conformity Thomas regarded as the most dangerous inhibitor of honest dissent because it worked in far more subtle and pervasive ways than the brute force of repression.

Thomas discussed his own experiences as a dissenter in an attempt to convince his readers that dissent was both personally and socially worthwhile. In reference to his political career, he said: "I certainly have not run repeatedly for office out of any masochistic pleasure in recurrent defeat."[26] Neither, he insisted, did he do so just to be in opposition or because of the expectation of election. Thomas indicated that he saw his candidacy as a means of furthering ". . .two related causes dear to my heart: the education of the public in democratic socialism and the realignment of American political parties so that our political divisions would be meaningful. . . ."[27] The relation in his thinking between dissent and constructive purpose is evident; but, in assessing his efforts, Thomas admitted that the results were mixed. He observed that his efforts at political realignment had failed and that "failure hurts." But "in respect to a certain degree of public education and a kind of indirect influence on the old parties, my failure was by no means so complete. I can honestly claim that something had been accomplished."[28]

Equally as important to Thomas as his success or failure was the enjoyment and satisfaction which he gained from his role as a dissenter. The dissenter's role gave him so much personal satisfaction because ". . .I would insist that to believe in something enough to stand on your own feet in its behalf, to feel that you are something more than a member of the herd, is a satisfaction transcending inescapable duty. You can find in it a real joy in life, especially if you hang on to a sense of humor."[29] The blend of principle and involvement which formed the basis of Thomas' love of dissent was the same one which motivated the rest of his reform activities. His sense of humor prevented his dissent from degenerating into fanaticism or crankiness.

Thomas concluded his article with a plea for the rise of a new kind of dissenter, one who would deny ". . .the notion that peace for my children and grandchildren can be guaranteed by the present race in arms."[30] He admitted the difficulty of dissenting against the centuries-old notion that peace could be maintained by preparing for war. However, the destructive potential of modern weapons was such that dissent against the traditional approach was essential. Thomas was hopeful in 1949 that the technique of dissent could be used to defend the principle of peace. As his subsequent activities and writings prove, he was one of the most persistent of the new dissenters who worked for peace.

In 1961, Thomas capped his lifelong interest in dissent with the publication of *Great Dissenters*. The volume is a series of essays in which Thomas, through material gleaned from standard biographies, assessed the contributions to mankind of such dissenters as Socrates, Galileo, Thomas Paine, Wendell Phillips, and Ghandi. In the introductory chapter, Thomas reiterated his belief in the virtues of dissent in terms which suggested his increased awareness of the need to balance it with conformity. The result was a more modest assessment of the significance of dissent, one which reflected Thomas' capacity to modify his assumptions in the face of new realities without surrendering his principles.

The definition and defense of dissent which he presented was a repetition of the ideas he had previously developed in his essays. He repeated the belief expressed in 1949 that ". . .heresy has always been the growing point of society, that our body politic always needs its Socratic gadflies, and that it forgets, disregards or suppresses its dissenters, past or present, at its peril."[31] He also repeated the argument originally developed in a 1959 essay that "The secret of a good life is to have the right loyalties and to hold them in the right scale of values. The value of dissent and dissenters is to make us reappraise those values with supreme concern for the truth."[32] Thomas' repetition of material previously developed in his essay in the *Great Dissenters* illustrates one of the major facets of his writings: all his books were broader expositions of ideas originally developed in his shorter writings about a given theme.

Thomas' introductory chapter made it clear that just as McCarthyism in America had sharpened his appreciation of dissent, so its demise had made him aware that a certain degree of conformity in a society was also necessary. He explained this transition in his thinking in the following words: "But as time went on and I considered my problem it became increasingly more complex than any stark contrast of black and white. On the one hand I became more conscious of the social values—even the necessity—of a high degree of conformity, if life is to be kept going, and on the other I found more uneasiness over our present type of American conformity, if not of significant dissent, than I had first assumed."[33] Conformity, Thomas realized, presented a certain degree of both personal and social security to individuals; for he was aware of the negative side of the dissenter's role. With typical Thomas frankness, he admitted that the dissenters whom he wrote about in his book would not have served as directors of the American Civil Liberties Union. Instead, "they would have claimed liberty to advance their truth so as—in many cases—to have liberty to enforce its acceptance on others."[34]

Faced with the conflicting demands of his traditional faith in dissent and his newly found awareness of the importance of reasonable conformity, Thomas fell back on a basic assumption. The subjects of his book ". . .were concerned as all worthwhile dissenters have been, not with dissent for its own sake, but only as necessary to advance the truth to which they were devoted."[35] That reason alone was sufficient cause for Thomas to celebrate the actions of the subjects of his book. Admiration for meaningful dissent remained one of the constants of Norman Thomas' civil libertarian thought.

III *Thomas and the Civil Rights Revolution*

The last two decades of Thomas' life were marked by the emergence of the Black Civil Rights Revolution. Thomas' passion for social justice and his unbending faith in the exalted place of civil liberties made it inevitable that he should become an active supporter of the struggle of Black Americans for full equality in American society in the 1950's and 1960's. Two examples of his writing, one in 1956 and the other in 1963, portray this aspect of Thomas' continuing commitment to the struggle for civil liberties in the closing years of his career. Both examples reflect his belief in the necessity of positive action rather than passive respect for civil liberties as well as his growing concern about what would occur if Black Americans did not achieve full equality. Finally, the two examples clearly illustrate the way Thomas used his writing as an integral part of his reform activities.

The first example was an open letter to President Dwight D. Eisenhower dated September 6, 1956, which appeared in

Thomas' syndicated newspaper column.[36] The letter was written during the period of violent resistance in parts of the South against attempts to integrate the public schools which resulted from the *Brown* v. *Board of Education of Topeka* school desegregation decision by the Supreme Court. Thomas' letter was an outright attempt to enlist the full powers of the presidency in the struggle for civil rights. Stating that ". . .I owe it to him to send him a copy of what I have written," Thomas, with characteristic candor, requested that his friend Maxwell M. Rabb, Secretary of the Cabinet, personally give a copy of his letter to the President.[37]

Thomas began his letter with praise of Eisenhower's recent press conference statements of his belief in the equality of men and the collective responsibility of Americans for enforcing laws which guaranteed it.[38] It was apparent from Thomas' remarks that he felt it was the chief executive's constitutional and moral duty not only to speak out but actually to enforce the court decision in the school desegregation case: "Under our constitution, which guarantees rights to the humblest of our citizens, the ultimate responsibility for enforcing a Supreme Court order which is systematically defied would fall, as you said, on yourself."[39] Thomas saw the vast potential which the weight of presidential power and prestige could give to the struggle for racial equality, and he was anxious that it be used to its fullest extent.

In an attempt to add weight to his call for presidential activism on behalf of civil rights, Thomas mentioned the impact of the issue on world opinion. He reminded the President that ". . .your conduct of foreign policy is terribly handicapped by reports of these riots with which a radio commentator from Moscow says 'the Russian propagandists are having a field day.' "[40] The obvious implication of Thomas' remark was that only strong executive action in support of the enforcement of desegregation could improve this situation. Speaking candidly, Thomas took serious issue with President Eisenhower's reference to "extremists on both sides" in the desegregation controversy: "Unfortunately, that expression is too often understood as apportioning guilt about equally between the aggressive segregationists and the advocates of obedience to the order of the Court. What seems to me worthy of all praise is the extraordinary self-control of our Negro fellow citizens and their avoidance of violence even in the face of provocation. . . . I take this method of respectfully asking whether it would not be a matter of simple justice for you publicly to acknowledge this restraint of a race whose dignity and patience in the face of persecution is worthy of all praise."[41] The patience of the Black man and the obvious justice of his cause had moved Thomas to take to task the President of the United States.

His passion for civil liberties caused Thomas to forget that the office of the American presidency was not essentially a moral one and that presidents, like all men, were shaped by the demands of politics and by their past. There was little in Eisenhower's background that worked to create empathy in him for the Civil Rights Revolution which exploded into public consciousness during his presidency. It should not seem surprising, however, that Thomas viewed the crisis over school desegregation as an essentially moral one. He concluded his plea to the President by reminding him that the human rights at stake in the crisis were part of a national moral issue which transcended regional political considerations.

To prove his point, he catalogued a long list of other aspects of American life where segregation was still powerfully entrenched: "Only recently, it has been emphatically called to my attention that there are towns in the North which allow no Negro to live in them, and that the fine stand of the churches at the national level has by no means ended Jim Crowism in the House of God. The uncompromising stand of the leaders of the AFL-CIO in support of the Supreme Court decision still leaves their organization with a great many local unions segregated solely on color lines. . . . It is this situation which makes your leadership for justice so important."[42] Thomas and many others were to be bitterly disappointed by the President's equivocation in the face of what they regarded as a clear-cut moral issue.

The second example of his writing in support of civil rights for Blacks was the statement which he submitted before a House of Representatives committee on July 26, 1963, in support of a proposed civil rights bill.[43] Thomas first attempted to create a proper mood of respect for his testimony by pointing out that the Socialist party had been one of the "main pioneers" of social justice in the United States and that many of the reforms which they had originally advocated had since become law.[44] He then turned to the subject of civil rights by saying: "The Socialist Party has long regarded civil rights as the Nation's leading domestic problem. We have seen it as the area of American life most desperately in need of a great act of national conscience. . . . That some progress has been made seems to us as impossible to deny as it is useless to proclaim. For the amount of progress has been ridiculously minute when placed alongside the size of the problem."[45] The battle against segregation was one which required a national moral commitment. He urged Congress to take decisive action to satisfy what he was convinced were the just demands of Black people.

He discussed what he felt would happen if Congress evaded its responsibility by passing "high-sounding but meaningless" legislation. Speaking frankly with what proved to be a great deal of foresight, he warned: "Such a course will only result in deep frustration out of which will come a mood of disbelief in the very method of legislative action as a way of remedying the ugly injustices that exist. That mood, in turn, will strengthen the irrational, racist, and authoritarian tendencies already in existence in embryonic form in the Negro community."[46] Thomas, who was aware of the growing mood of frustration in the Black community before many other leaders, clearly sensed that it could lead to violence. The sense of alarm evident in Thomas' warning to Congress was not present in his earlier letter to President Eisenhower. Sensitivity to the changing mood of Black Americans had greatly reinforced his earlier belief in the need for prompt national attention to eliminate racial discrimination.

Urging rapid congressional action, Thomas recommended a whole series of steps which he hoped would be included in an all-out attack on racial discrimination. He criticized President Kennedy's proposal that the federal government be permitted to withhold funds from any activity where discrimination occurs because such a method did not go far enough. Thomas urged, instead, that it be replaced by an immediate executive order banning federal support of all segregated activities.

Next, he summarized the role which economic discrimination played in denying equal opportunity to the Black man and called for a concerted attack on it. He repeated the belief which he had expressed in his earlier letter to Eisenhower about the nationwide existence of racism, but he then emphasized that this fact was no excuse to take pressure and blame off the South where, he was convinced, the most widespread and direct violations of civil liberties occurred. He indicated his awareness of another important aspect of the problem when he added: "Yet it is precisely because northern Negroes are free of the most primitive forms of Jim Crow but find themselves nonetheless exploited and denied equal opportunity that the northern situation is potentially most explosive."[47]

Thomas concluded by proposing a three-point plan to overcome the economic aspects of segregation which included a national fair employment practices board, large-scale apprenticeship programs for Blacks, and a large-scale public works program for Black unskilled workers.[48] The comprehensiveness of Thomas' proposals symbolized his growing awareness in the 1960's of the complex collection of forces which reinforced racial discrimination in American life. His testimony on behalf of the Civil Rights Bill of 1963 indicated his continued faith in the value of strong governmental support of the attack on segregation, particularly its ability to attack the economic aspects of racism. He hoped it would serve as the spearhead of a comprehensive attack on all forms of segregation.

IV *Conclusion: The Return to Fundamentals*

The chapter entitled "Toward Civil Liberties and Civil Rights" in Thomas' posthumously published *The Choices* is a fitting summary of the civil libertarian principles which he developed and applied during his lifetime.[49] In it, he underscores his conviction that civil libertarianism, like the other aspects of his reform thought, involved fundamental moral questions. He reiterates his faith that the preservation of civil liberties would guarantee the dignity of the individual which he cherished so highly. He reinforces the previously developed thesis that his civil libertarianism was the product of the interaction of fundamental humanistic values and the experience of his activism.

The first part of the chapter is a discussion of the nature of civil rights and their proper application. Thomas recalled some remarks by a policeman who had arrested him during a demonstration in New Jersey in 1926. The policeman had expressed confusion because some things that people did were moral and not legal while others were legal and not moral. Thomas felt that the point which the policeman had raised was relevant when applied to questions about civil liberties because it exemplified the philosophically unsound tendency to divide law from morality when discussing civil rights. Civil liberties involved legal and moral assumptions which were inextricably intertwined. Thus, Thomas explained, "The right to speak, to vote, to sit where you choose in a bus are all expressions of the rights an individual in the United States of 1968 must have if he is to possess the human dignity of a man."[50] Individual freedoms were to be protected by law because they were the basis of human dignity, a concept defined in terms of moral judgments. Thomas was confident that man could build a society where there would be no conflict between law and morality if both were used to protect human dignity.

Despite his belief in their importance, Thomas emphasized that the exercise of civil liberties could not be carried to the point of anarchy. He recognized that the problem of balancing personal freedom with social order was a continuing one, an ". . .illustration of the difficulties with absolutes."[51] In typical Thomas style, he presented a number of practical examples which justified the need for a pragmatic approach to the problem. Driving on the wrong side of the road and rejecting society's right to protect itself by vaccination were, in Thomas' view, unrealistic exercises of individual freedom which society could not tolerate. Laws restricting libel, the open circulation of pornography, and attempts at violent revolutions did not violate freedoms of speech, press, and association. The use of such examples enabled him to illustrate effectively the fallacies of basing civil liberties on absolutist standards. Instead, as in his earlier discussions, he sought to justify them in terms of their pragmatic social value.

The same assumptions which appeared originally in

Thomas' writings on conscription and conscientious objection during World War I characterized his discussion of American involvement in Vietnam. He expressed anew his belief that conscription for military duty was ". . .the strongest imaginable assertion of the right of society to equality of service at the expense of the individual—regardless of his own principles."[52] America, he reminded his readers, had a long tradition of resistance to the draft though it had been mostly dormant since World War I. The renewed growth of resistance to the draft on grounds of conscience during the Vietnam conflict delighted Thomas; and he praised Dr. Benjamin Spock, the Rev. William Sloane Coffin, Jr., Mitchell Goodman, and others who had been indicted for advising students to refuse the draft on grounds of conscience. He defended them by referring to both American and international precedents for their behavior. He cited the operation of the Underground Railroad during the American Civil War and the decision of the International Court at the Nuremberg Trial at the end of World War II which stated that individuals should have disobeyed the German laws rather than commit crimes against humanity.

After denying the workability of the absolutist approach to civil libertarianism, Thomas emphasized that his belief in balance should not be construed too narrowly. He considered it imperative that a democracy not prevent the theoretical discussion of issues, even those that included ". . .an advocacy of ultimate violence unless certain things are done."[53] He justified this attitude with the argument that history had proven that it was better to treat those advocating future violence with discussion and debate rather than repression. Again, Thomas fell back on one of the basic tenets of his civil libertarian faith—that heresy was a major cause of social progress. As he put it: "We can risk listening to many extreme opinions, to many false prophets if we have time to answer them by word or deed."[54] Dissent, by his reasoning, should only be inhibited when it constituted a "clear and present danger" to society.

Thomas admitted that there had been real progress in the struggle for civil liberties in his lifetime even though ". . .there has not been and perhaps never can be a final victory in this area."[55] He noted that there was far more tolerance of freedom of speech, press, and association during the Vietnam

War than in previous American wars. There was, however, one aspect of the war which had created renewed debate and even civil disobedience: the argument over conscientious objection to the draft.

Using his discussion of the war in Vietnam as a point of departure, Thomas presented a general discussion of the values of civil disobedience. He reminded his readers that there was one ethical question underlying all the various kinds of civil disobedience practiced in modern America: where did man's ultimate loyalties lie? In discussing that question, Thomas emphasized that he was not a believer in civil disobedience *per se* because it could be used to justify any particular whim a person had. He was disturbed because there was ". . .too much civil disobedience defended by well-paid, high-powered attorneys. . ." for such things as nonpayment of taxes for political reasons or the violation of prohibition laws because of a desire to drink.[56]

For Thomas, civil disobedience was justified only in those rare instances when an individual's freedom of conscience was violated. It was never to be used, as in the case of some American student radicals, as the means of perpetrating violent confrontations or creating wanton destruction. Civil disobedience, to Norman Thomas, was a last-ditch defense of an individual's freedom of conscience; and it was to be used by moral men for moral reasons.

Thomas concluded his discussion of civil rights in *The Choices* by expressing his approval that they were guaranteed by the Constitution. He hastened to add, however, that ". . .the moral case for these rights and liberties is not derived from the Constitution. It is derived from the kind of thinking so well expressed by Thoreau in his *Essay on Civil Disobedience,* which he wrote in opposition to the Mexican War: There come times in life when our conception of our duties may be determined by the conviction that we ought to obey God, rather than man."[57] Norman Thomas ended his exposition of civil liberties at the same point where he had begun fifty years before defending the priorities of conscience over the demands of the state. His civil libertarianism, like Thoreau's, was anchored on his moral concept of the worth of man. His writings on civil liberties reveal this point most clearly.

CHAPTER 7

The Search for Peace in a Hostile World

THE third major theme in Thomas' writing was his plea for peace. Like the other themes in his writing, it continued to be a goal of his reform efforts throughout his career. So also like them, it was characterized by one central assumption: in this case, the absolute necessity of eliminating war as a means of resolving human conflict. The discussion of peace in his essays and books is, in effect, a record of Norman Thomas' often frustrating search for alternatives to war in the face of the rapidly changing events of this century. As a result, this study of the essential ideas which Thomas developed in his search for peace and the context in which they developed seeks to illustrate the major lines of continuity and change in his thinking by an examination of selected examples of his writings from different periods of his career. The topical-chronological divisions in this chapter are based on the remarkably candid assessment of his work for peace which appeared in the last chapter of his 1951 volume, *A Socialist's Faith.*[1]

The recurring references to peace in the midst of his discussions of his other major themes and his increasing preoccupation with the means of achieving it in his later years suggest that he came to regard the creation of a world without war as the most important of his reform goals. For this reason, the chapter is a fitting conclusion to the study of the major themes in Norman Thomas' writings.

I *From the First World War to the 1930's: The Dominance of Pacifism*

The core of Thomas' writing on peace in the first two decades of his reform career was his exposition of pacifism. In pacifism, he saw the means to break the age-old cycle of dependence on violence as the ultimate way of resolving conflict among humans. Recalling in 1951 his search for peace in the early phase of his career, Thomas said: "World War I drove me, at that time an active Christian clergyman, to examine the problem of Christianity and the *method* of war, whatever the objective. I was constrained to accept Christian pacifism."[2] This attitude caused him to defend conscientious objectors during World War I and to regard them as true prophets of a world without war.

An excellent exposition of the fundamental assumptions behind his early pacifism appeared in an essay entitled "Is Violence the Way?" in the May, 1919, issue of *The World Tomorrow.*[3] There, Thomas revealed the same combination of idealism and realism which characterized all of his reform writings. The first part of the article is a discussion of what was to become a major feature of Thomas' reform thought: the demand for consistency of means and ends. Emphasizing the irony of mankind's enduring faith in the possibility of a better world and his persistent failure to attain it, he noted: "For this failure one of the most significant reasons, too commonly ignored in our thinking, is our excessive preoccupation with results rather than methods. We have eyes only for the goal and so miss the road. What we desire always seems to matter more than how we seek it."[4] The emphasis of ends over means was, he felt, often reinforced by the pressure for social conformity. As he explained, "*Individuals* may hesitate at the use of certain means; *social groups* whether organized on racial or class lines feel themselves exempt from considerations which might restrain individuals."[5] As an example, he told how the same clergymen who had condemned violence by exploited workers in labor disputes prior to the war had come to regard our war against Germany as a blessed crusade against evil. In this manner, Thomas illustrated how ". . .a passionate devotion to a cause makes most men lose their horror even of such a method [wholesale slaughter] if they feel they must employ it to gain their end."[6] Such was the tragedy of an overemphasis on ends as opposed to means.

The second part of the article was a discussion of the lesson which he felt World War I held for mankind. He began with a chilling remark: "Some day a genius may arise who—unless he first goes mad with horror of what it has been given him to understand—will clothe in deathless form a record not only of the inferno of the War, but of its infinite cost to humanity."[7] Thomas then catalogued the appalling cost of the war in both human and physical terms. After listing the estimated number dead from combat, massacre, famine, and disease, he pointed out the weakening effect of the war on man's moral fiber. With characteristic irony, Thomas reminded his readers that: "And all this is the aftermath of a war of liberation, avowedly waged in behalf of humanity."[8]

The third part of the article was a discussion of the alternatives to violence in which Thomas reiterated his plea for the moral consistency of ends and means. He emphasized that the changed attitude toward violence had to come from within, and he urged that it be based on "love of comrades," the desire to improve the condition of mankind because "With that 'dear love of comrades' the organized violence of war, of terrorism, of bloody revolution is inevitably incompatible unless we are to be guilty of using our fellow beings. . .as things to be manipulated or devils to be destroyed."[9] Such a concept of human brotherhood, if practiced, would guarantee nonviolence. This aspect of Thomas' argument reveals his heavy reliance early in his career on the importance of individual decisions as the basis of reform. While he never completely renounced this emphasis, his later writings treat individual decisions as only one of a group of necessary prerequisites for peace.

Thomas found additional support for his argument about the consistency of ends and means as a deterrent to violence in the teachings of the great moral teachers in the Christian tradition: "The glory of the greatest of our spiritual leaders, of Jesus, of Francis of Assisi, of Tolstoi, is a certain majestic simplicity of ethical teaching and practise. To hate and to kill are wrong. The Kingdom of heaven is not for men of violence but for little children. The way of life is the way of love."[10] Why then did men find it hard to apply such clear-cut principles with a consistent use of ends and means? Could it be that such consistent teachings were inapplicable in the complex real world? Addressing himself to those who claimed that wars were necessary to overcome oppression and defend brotherhood, Thomas said: "Wars and bloody revolutions have ended ancient oppressions and given freedom room for nobler growth; but is it not the outstanding tragedy of history that the results are so out of proportion to the unselfish idealism of the heroes who have perished sword in hand?"[11] He was convinced that a better way existed.

Thomas insisted that man did possess a viable alternative to violence, one that would confine its extent and limit hate: passive resistance. In describing it, he said: "Men have almost uniformly rejected the method of passive resistance, but it is a matter of sober fact that when they have tried it the results have been astonishing. The blood of martyrs has been the fruitful seed of the progress and freedom of mankind."[12] His firsthand observation of a small number of conscientious objectors defying the coercive power of the American military system made him confident that passive resistance could be the basis of a new approach to the resolution of human conflict.

To Thomas, the success of such a method, however, was ultimately dependent on man's ability to change human nature. As his following remarks reveal, he was fully aware of the challenge confronting those who sought such a change: "There are ways abstractly more efficient than war. The difficulty is that by virtue of every instinct, of a heritage that goes back to the beginning of time, violence is the natural accompaniment of men's struggle alike for freedom or for power."[13] Despite the difficulties, Thomas was confident that human nature could be changed; and he placed his hope in Christianity as the vehicle through which such a change could be accomplished.[14] He saw in its call for a new social order based on Christ's teachings the means to abolish violence. Christian pacifism was the basis of Norman Thomas' search for peace.

To say that Thomas' writing on peace in the first two decades of his career was dominated by his devotion to pacifism is not to suggest that it was stagnant. It reflects, instead, his growing awareness of the immense complexity of the problems confronting those who sought to create a world without war. Writing in *The World Tomorrow* in January, 1924, Thomas presented a broadened concept of the types of activism which he felt would be effective in the search for peace.[15] This and other articles clearly indicate that the movement away from reliance on pacifism as a sole means of achieving peace was an evolutionary process, one born of Thomas' increased exposure to new realities.

The 1924 article is an assessment of the movement for the outlawry of war by legal means which became highly popular in the mid-1920's.[16] His general reaction to that approach was one of skepticism: "In short, there is no patent medicine, neither the outlawry of war, nor any other, which will cure the ills of the acquisitive society. There is no one peace plan. The problem of peace is a problem of education. It includes the culture of the international mind, a revolutionized teaching of history, a better perception of what war really means."[17] Thomas was very much concerned lest those who worked for peace adopt a too simplistic approach in their attempt to achieve this goal.

He concluded his essay with a summation of what he felt were the four principal problems confronting those who wished to rid the world of war. The first which he discussed was the problem of economic inequity. It was important that the peoples of the world ". . .learn to use the marvelous resources of the earth and the wealth of human skill cooperatively for the sake of life more abundant rather than profit more abounding."[18] The second problem was political disagreement which Thomas hoped to solve with "more open diplomacy." The third which he emphasized was the "personal and spiritual" crisis. Means would have to be developed to get individuals to utterly refuse to take part in war because it was ". . .beyond the pale of decency, humanity and truth."[19] The final problem was the presence of injustice. Against this, Thomas urged groups to ". . .experiment in non-violent means of resistance to injustice."[20]

His concluding remark left no doubt as to which of the approaches he felt was most important: "It is this perfection of methods of 'non-violent coercion' which seems to me most important to lovers of peace confronted with the hideous evils of our present-day world."[21] His writing clearly indicates that Thomas, though he broadened his approach to the problem of peace in the fifteen years after World War I, still regarded pacifism and the nonviolence which was its corollary as the most important of the approaches to peace.[22] Thomas was certain that peace could only be obtained by those who practiced nonviolence. The events of the mid-1930's that would cause him to surrender his pacifism were yet to come.

II *The Impact of Totalitarianism: The Surrender of Pacifism and the Rejection of Collective Security*

The rise of totalitarian dictatorships in the 1930's affected Thomas' approach to peace just as deeply as it did his thinking on Socialism and civil liberties. Thomas' writing reflects his growing awareness of the threat which totalitarianism posed for the peaceful world he hoped to create. It records the agonizing reappraisal which led him to surrender his pacifism and the reasons for his refusal to join those who advocated collective security against the totalitarian states. Above all, it reminds his readers that, despite the surrender of his pacifism, Thomas never lost sight of his basic goal—a world without war.

As for the particular factors that caused Thomas to change his approach, two statements from his 1951 book, *A Socialist's Faith,* are most revealing. In reference to his surrender of absolute pacifism in the 1930's, Thomas said: "But in a world wholly unready for that high endeavor, it does not, I think, make for the triumph of justice or peace to preach a political program of pacifism which practically would mean surrender to brutal totalitarian might."[23] Experience, the same factor which had already caused Thomas to broaden his approach to peace in the 1920's, caused him to abandon pacifism in the 1930's. It simply was not an adequate weapon in the face of the Fascists' willingness to use any method to achieve their ends.

This decision did not, however, drive Thomas into the camp of those who advocated the use of collective security against Germany, Italy, and Japan. Instead, as he explained, his ". . .reluctant rejection of pacifism if anything intensified my sense of the horror and futility of the method of total war."[24] The short-range advantages of collective security were far outweighed by this consideration. Thomas' rejection of both pacifism and collective security forced him to search for a viable alternative.

The accuracy of Thomas' later explanation of the transitions in his approach to peace in the later 1930's is substantiated by an examination of his writing during that period. One particularly good indication of the state of Thomas' thought was his article, "The Pacifist's Dilemma," which appeared in the January 16, 1937, issue of *The Nation.*[25] In it, he discussed both his surrender of pacifism and his rejection of collective security. The agony that Thomas experienced as the war clouds gathered in Europe is evident in the opening words of his essay. There, he used the actions of President Roosevelt—whom he noted was a proponent of the naval-arms race who had just returned from a good-will tour of the Western Hemisphere and condemned the sale of weapons to the recognized Spanish government—to illustrate the confused state of world affairs. The upshot of that confusion was that "Rarely. . .has the struggle for peace been so complicated, or have the lovers of peace been more sharply divided. They are caught in the confusion of a world more keenly aware than ever before of the suicidal costs of world war, yet more inclined to accept it as inevitable."[26] The pessimism and irony in Thomas' remarks are evident.

Thomas regarded the basic cause of the confusing situation which confronted those working for peace in the 1930's to be the triumph of Fascism in Germany, Italy, and Japan and the subsequent glorification of militarism and war in those states. To illustrate its confusing impact, he made reference to the Spanish Civil War: "One may be against both war and fascism, and yet find in every dispatch from Spain grim proof that practically, under conditions all too likely to occur again and again, resolute and effective opposition to fascism means war."[27] Small wonder that the pacifists were divided. Thomas was convinced that the nature of Fascism was such that it presented a choice of submission to slavery or to war. Fascism contained devastating implications for Thomas' belief in the need for a consistent moral relationship between ends and means.

Thomas then critically described and discussed the positions of ". . .two groups which at first sight seem more consistent than the rest of us" in their opposition to war and Fascism.[28] He characterized the two groups with the following words:

"There are on the one hand those pacifists who hold that the great commandment can be summed up in this: 'Thou shalt take no part in any kind of war.' On the other hand there are those advocates of collective security who proclaim a holy crusade of democratic nations against fascist aggressors."[29] The impact of Fascism had driven the supporters of peace in two directions, neither of which was realistic to Thomas.

Turning first to the pacifists, he described their position in terms that proved he no longer regarded their position as valid; but he also reminded his readers that there "are pacifists and pacifists." The pacifists whom Thomas most respected emphasized that history bore out the futility of war as a means of resolving human conflict. He admitted as sound in the context of the era their arguments that favored Americans bringing about a negotiated peace during World War I, that the Peace of Versailles was unrealistic, and that German democracy should have been supported in its struggle against militarism. However, Thomas asserted, "Today these pacifists can make no equally practical suggestion in the struggle against fascist aggression, but at least we owe them something for their constant challenge to the method of war and their constant reminder of its bitter cost."[30] In this manner, Thomas paid a fitting tribute to his former pacifism while at the same time emphasizing the inadequacy of that position because of the Fascist threat.

The approach which Thomas took to collective security, a position which he had never supported, was far less sympathetic. He simply reiterated the arguments which he had been using against the concept since World War I. He noted that the advocates of collective security who had originally called for the unification of the whole world against the aggressor nations had hoped that the threat of overwhelming military power and economic sanctions would deter them. However, they had recently changed their approach to one that relied on an alliance of just the "democratic" states against the dictators. Thomas regarded this narrower approach as important because it ". . .signifies the historical failure of collective security through the League of Nations."[31]

He then cited the indecisive and varied reactions of the capitalist democracies to the Spanish Civil War to prove the futility of depending on their unifying against Fascism. Such an approach, he argued, overlooked the fact that Fascism was ". . .a logical stage of development of the ideals and institutions of capitalism and nationalism. They made the first world war. They made the peace of Versailles. They plowed the soil in which Hitler sowed the seeds of his tribal fascism."[32] It was important to remember that "Loyalty to democracy, even bourgeois democracy, may well be invoked in the struggle against fascism. But at best it can only win a temporary victory. The essential struggle is still socialism against capitalism, not democracy against fascism."[33] No better illustration exists than this statement of the close relationship between his work for Socialism and his work for peace. One of the fundamental prerequisites for a peaceful world was the creation of a Socialist one.

Thomas concluded by discussing the implications of his rejection of pacifism and collective security for Americans. He emphasized that American neutrality should not prevent American volunteers from going to Spain to fight for democracy if they so wished, and that the Spanish Republican government should not be denied the supplies necessary to put down the Fascist rebellion against it.[34] However, he was also certain that "It is far more feasible for the workers and all lovers of peace to try to keep America out of the pursuit of war profits and hence out of war, and in the comparative sanity of this condition to see that it uses its influence for peace."[35] Thomas hoped to use American non-involvement as the basis of a lasting peace, as was apparent in his assertion that "Not a method of keeping out of war but the establishment of a warless world must be our goal."[36]

One of the best discussions of Thomas' hopes for America appeared in his 1938 book, *Socialism on the Defensive.*[37] In it, Thomas argued that America, because of her fortunate geographic position, had a chance to stay out of the war. Staying out was important because it gave the United States a chance to ". . .preserve the democracy which we have."[38] He was certain that American entry into the war would result in the death of democracy because the country would succumb to the temptation to use the same methods as its enemies to achieve victory. Peace would provide ". . .socialism—as contrasted with any kind of totalitarianism—a chance of resuming its aggressive campaign for the achievement of the good society through the fellowship of free men."[39] Thomas saw America as the best hope for world peace because it was the most secure place to build the cooperative commonwealth which would do away with war.

Such reasoning caused the American Socialist party under Thomas' leadership to stand alone among the Socialist parties affiliated with the Second Socialist International against the reliance on collective security as a defense against Fascism. This stand caused Friedrich Adler, the Secretary of the International, to condemn Thomas' position: "Norman Thomas' group destroyed the basis of true internationalism with their ultra pacifism and isolationism."[40] Unmoved by such criticisms, Thomas maintained his position until the Japanese attack on Pearl Harbor forced the United States into World War II.

The crucial point to remember is that Thomas advocated this position for different reasons than the majority of the isolationists of the period. They desired the preservation of the *status quo,* but Thomas was convinced that an America at peace could be the basis of a new order of things. His writing proves that both his and the isolationists' calls for American non-involvement were the product of coincidence rather than of similarity of motives. His activities during World War II substantiated this point.

III *World War II: The Search for a Lasting Peace*

American entry into World War II after the attack on Pearl Harbor forced Thomas to give up his hopes for a plan of peace premised on non-involvement. Again, as with his surrender of pacifism in the face of the Fascist threat of the 1930's, Thomas was forced to modify his search for peace because of new realities. Writing later in his book, *A Socialist's Faith,* he recalled his reaction to the American entry into the war. "I, the hater of war, chose as between circles of hell. I chose critical but active support of the war to a point where a decent peace might be possible. For that end I worked inside and outside the Socialist Party."[41] Norman Thomas devoted the war years to the struggle for the "decent peace," and his writing reflects his preoccupation with the things necessary to assure permanent and lasting peace. His publications also indicate that the American entry into the war hastened the formulation of his specific plan for peace in the post-war world.

The pamphlet, *World Federation: What Are the Difficulties?*, which he published in 1942 while he was chairman of The Post War World Council, provides an excellent summation of the seminal ideas underlying his work for peace during this period.[42] In it, Thomas began by noting the popularity of plans based on post-war world cooperation and world government. He cautioned that such plans would come to naught if they were premised on the traditional demands of power politics. Instead, he urged men to ". . .think and plan in terms of world-wide well-being. . ." which would have to be built on a "new framework for peace."[43] The events since World War I had convinced Thomas that some means must be found to place moral law above national sovereignty.

After expressing his support for a world federation of nations, Thomas presented a frank discussion of the obstacles and awesome tasks confronting those who wished to implement that approach to peace. One of the major things which he saw as working against the achievement of world federation was the "loose thinking and loose talking" about the possibility of world government. Such talk, he felt, created the image of a highly centralized world state in which the American people would be asked to place their fate in a system in which they would be outnumbered by Chinese, Indians, and Russians. The impact of such a plan in the United States would be such that "The storm which was successfully raised against Woodrow Wilson's League of Nations would be a zephyr compared with the tornado of opposition which would sweep away any idea of world government as the man in the street and the election booth would be made to understand that phrase."[44] History had provided Thomas with a convincing argument against the possibility of any American acceptance of a centralized world government.

Even if the proposed world government could survive American domestic opposition, Thomas saw an even more crucial flaw in such a plan: the idea of world government was intimately related to the old power politics. Such a world government would have to be imposed by a "league of victors." Thomas expressed doubt that such a league would be either strong enough or well enough united to impose world-wide rule. Moreover, to operate in any form, ". . .such a government would have to be a military dictatorship. . . . To impose a world state on existing states, if it were successful, would be the end of liberty."[45] Thus, Thomas added a second basic argument against those who proposed a world government. For these reasons, Thomas regarded the creation of a world government based on highly centralized control as "inconceivable."

Having rejected the viability of world government, Thomas then explained his concept of a world federation. He emphasized that ". . .successful federation. . .requires us to find the minimum, not the maximum, concessions which our own and other nations should make to whatever League or any other central agency may be set up."[46] Thomas regarded his approach as far more realistic in the face of the power of nationalism in the modern world. As an example, he pointed out that he saw ". . .no parallels in the present day experiences of our divided world" to the "aids to union" which the Americans had experienced in their Declaration of Independence, Revolutionary War, and the creation of the national domain out of the Western lands.[47] The lack of such a world-wide consensus meant that the search for basic agreement had to be cautious. There was no common ideology upon which the federationists could build. One had only to contrast the governments and cultures of the major nations of the world to grasp this point.

What did Thomas feel would be the "minimum concessions" which would make such a federation possible? Forswearing even his beloved Democratic Socialism, he asserted: "Hence it has become my conviction that the most that can possibly be required of nations comprising a federation is abstention from aggression abroad and from the persecution of cultural and other minorities within their borders."[48] Thomas' approach thus began with an assumption that the supporters of world government held as their goal. He would create a cessation of hostilities as a beginning and then build the means to preserve it. The "minimum concession" cited by Thomas symbolized a basic shift in his thinking about the means to achieve both peace and Socialism. Formerly, he had insisted that peace would come only after the creation of a federation of Democratic Socialist commonwealths. The rise of Fascism and the war itself had convinced him that the safety of democracy and Socialism would never be assured unless the "war system" was destroyed first.

Thomas was certain that the minimum concessions cited above would not in themselves insure the success of a world federation in the post-war years. Noting that "The one passion which men will share in common is a passion for peace," Thomas pointed out that those favoring the federation would have to prove that it could prevent future wars.[49] Thus, it was important that the builders of the federation avoid the mistakes of the past.

Thomas felt that a federation based on the minimum rather than the maximum concessions of power by the nations involved would provide the necessary flexibility for the peaceful resolution of conflicts. What he regarded as the major error of the Versailles Treaty, the creation of little states "claiming absolute sovereignty," would be solved by grouping such nations into closely knit regional federations which would in turn join his world federation. The successful development of cooperation which resulted from the social services of the League of Nations would be continued and enlarged. The League's greatest failure, its emphasis on the defense of an "unsatisfactory status quo," would be corrected by revision of international agreements.[50] Thomas predicated his approach on his belief that the mistakes of the past provided practical lessons for the future.

As for the means by which his proposed world federation would enforce the peace, Thomas emphasized that one thing was crucial: ". . .the most obvious requirement. . .is that it possess the sole armed force likely to be in any way sufficient for modern war."[51] Well aware of the dangers implicit in giving any sovereign entity such an important power, he emphasized that it should be granted only after the fulfillment of "two broad, general conditions," both of which would be hard to fill. Those conditions were:

1. Assurance to all peoples that the central military police power will not be aggressively used by any sort of political combination against any particular nation.
2. The provision of political and economic machinery as an effective alternative to war in adjusting grievances and giving to all peoples an approximate equality of right and opportunity.[52]

He was confident that these general principles would limit both the means and the excuse for nations to resort to violence. He felt that such an approach was realistic because it eliminated what he regarded as the real causes of war.

Continuing, he explained that the rapid implementation of a world federation for peace would by its nature spare the world the dangers implicit in either a prolonged armistice or the return of America to isolationism. He saw both of these conditions as increasing the chances for a third world war. A long armistice at the end of World War II would inevitably lead to increasing quarrels among the victors, to steadily increasing irritation among the peoples policed by the victors, and to the development of imperialism and militarism within the victor nations.[53] Isolation, argued Thomas, would not permit ". . .the United States to go about its business in a world rent by hunger, hate and war."[54] Any attempt to stand aloof would, in the long run, lead not only to American involvement but also, because of our participation in two world wars, to suspicion about its eventual intentions. His warning about the dangers of an extended post-war truce proved to be prophetic.

The conclusion of the pamphlet was a reiteration of Thomas' belief in the importance of using moral means to achieve moral ends: "The war system is a world-wide affair. It should be conquered by a world-wide peace system. The very fact that such a system will never evolve by a natural process out of war, no matter who is the victor, is the more reason for all of us who love peace to concern ourselves with plans appropriate to it."[55] Though persuaded that the odds against the creation of a world federation for peace were great, Thomas urged his readers to work for the acceptance of a plan which ". . .may redeem them and their children from the curse of war."[56] He considered the struggle for such a goal imperative, regardless of the odds.

Having examined the basic assumptions which he presented in his pamphlet, it is easy to see why Thomas found much that disturbed him in the Allied prosecution of the war and in the Allied plans for the post-war period. His later writings during the war were critical of the Allied decision to seek unconditional surrender of the Axis powers, the use of atomic weapons against Japan, and the big power domination of the proposed United Nations.[57] Thomas regarded these and many other actions as manifestations of the old power politics which had subverted the Peace of Versailles, encouraged the growth of Fascism, and led to World War II. Even more important, he saw them as potential causes of the mistrust which would lead eventually to a third world war.

The influence of both history and experience on Thomas' response to World War II is obvious in his writing. He viewed his proposed world federation as the only realistic substitute for the perpetuation of a system which relied on war as its ultimate means of resolving human conflict. Both the logic with which he justified his position in his writings and the events of the post-war years make it difficult to dismiss his call for a federation for peace as misguided idealism. Norman Thomas did present an alternative, and part of the tragedy of his life was that no one had the courage to test its validity.

IV *The Road to Peace in the Nuclear Age*

Writing in 1951 in *A Socialist's Faith,* Thomas said: "We cannot prove what might have been. We cannot live over again the years that are gone. We can learn from them. . . . But —and on this all men of good will must agree—our fairest chance of success lies in avoiding the method of war which, in two titanic conflicts fought before the atomic age and won by the better side, brought mankind so close to ruin."[58] With these words, Norman Thomas summarized the beliefs which made peace his "deepest concern" in the closing years of his life.[59] The dawning of the atomic age and the arms race which it spawned convinced him that mankind could not survive a third world war. Thus, his writings on peace in the post-war years reflect a sense of urgency that borders on desperation.

In 1959, Thomas published his book, *The Prerequisites for*

Peace, in which he presented both a rationale for and an outline of what he felt was a realistic plan for peace in a world dominated by the Cold War. The thesis of the book was the same one which he had propounded since the beginning of his crusade against war: "It is the thesis of this book that the logical reaction would lead to a very different policy of war prevention than our own or any other nation is following."[60] The most crucial of the mistakes which Thomas saw was the American willingness to rely on the "balance of terror" which resulted from the escalating arms race between the Communist bloc and the Western powers. Too many factors, including the possibility of an accident, caused him to reject the assumption of Henry Kissinger and others that nations, even when threatened with defeat, would refrain from using nuclear weapons because of their horrible destructive potential.[61]

Instead of arming, Thomas insisted, Americans could and should work for peace through the United Nations. Cognizant that the basic reason for Americans not doing so was their distrust of the Russians, Thomas reminded his readers that the face of Soviet Communism was changing and that the past memories of the Cold War would have to give way before new realities. After pointing out a series of changes occurring in the Soviet Union, including the increased emphasis on consumer-goods production and the weakening Soviet grip on its satellites, Thomas argued that "the facts of life" were steadily reducing the economic differences which separated capitalism and Communism as both were being practiced.[62] In this manner, he attempted to convince his readers that, while the Russians were certainly not to be regarded as friends, there were possibilities of achieving accommodation with them on important issues of mutual interest such as an approach to peace.

In an effort to develop more relative perspective among his readers, Thomas in a chapter entitled "But Can We Trust Ourselves?" pointed to a number of aspects of the Cold War in which American actions had worked against the cause of peace. Thomas emphasized that, although the Russians had started the Cold War, the United States had done little to prevent it. He characterized the negative aspects of American policy as including such things as the escalation of the arms race, the development of a neo-imperialism, and a lack of effort to strengthen the United Nations. As examples of American intransigence, he noted that much of the disagreement with the Russians in the United Nations was over procedural matters and that it was unrealistic for Americans to threaten war if the Russians established bases in the Caribbean while expecting her to do nothing about the many American bases near the Soviet borders. He also cited the alarming growth of the vested interest in the arms race symbolized by the development of the industrial-military complex as further proof that some Americans were deeply committed to the perpetuation of Cold War tensions.[63] Such conditions led Thomas to conclude that the American efforts to peace during the Cold War had been, at their very best, ambiguous.

Thomas then presented what he regarded as the fundamental "prerequisites" for peace. Emphasizing that there was no single all-encompassing plan, he cited three steps which he regarded as essential: disarmament, disengagement, and the strengthening of the United Nations as a peace-enforcing agency.[64] He developed what he felt were the major aspects of each of these steps in separate chapters; but, discussing disarmament first, he outlined three essentials which its advocates must demand of all governments of the world. These were acceptance of the idea that universal disarmament was the price of escape from nuclear war, an overall plan for disarmament applicable to conventional as well as nuclear weapons, and the prompt beginning of a first step.[65] Thomas was convinced that the way to disarm was to disarm and that the success of disarmament depended upon the workability of his other two prerequisites for peace.

The second major prerequisite, disengagement, symbolized the adjustment of Thomas' approach to peace caused by the bipolarization which characterized the Cold War. He first made sure that his readers understood that he did not mean isolation or withdrawal from the United Nations by his use of this term. He meant, rather, ". . .phased withdrawal of armed forces from a defined area to create a militarily neutralized belt or zone" and a ". . .withdrawal from, or at least critical clarification of, our national commitments to intervene in other nations' wars."[66] Disengagement was a means of cooling off the tensions created by the Cold War.

Thomas' proposals for the strengthening of the United Nations centered on a group of charter amendments that would vastly enlarge the peacekeeping responsibilities of the world organization. In forming them, he admittedly borrowed heavily from Grenville Clark and Louis Sohn's book, *World Peace Through World Law.*[67] Some of the more important changes which Thomas proposed were laws against violence, courts to interpret them, and a police force to enforce them. In terms which reflected his faith that violence could be legislated out of existence only if its causes were removed, he urged the creation of machinery to remove the vast economic disparities which he regarded as the primary cause of instability in the world.[68]

In concluding, Thomas reminded his readers that he had written *The Prerequisites for Peace* to suggest attainable goals for those who worked for peace. He admitted that the obstacles confronting those who sought the elimination of war were massive. Particularly challenging was the "...fixed idea on both sides of the cold war that sooner or later what the enemy claims is for his defense will be used by him for aggression" which made it "...difficult to get a sustained and intelligent...interest in the processes of disarmament and disengagement on which war or peace depend."[69] Despite this mistrust, Thomas was confident that the growing world awareness that nuclear war could lead to annihilation served as a motivating force for peace. He was certain that such groups as the Socialists, trade unions, churches, and other organizations could develop a "dynamics of peace" if given the proper leadership.[70] The price of failure made such positive action for peace imperative.

In this manner, Thomas sought to provide a viable alternative to the Cold War and the arms race. In so doing, he emphasized the need for a change in human attitudes toward war, one of the earliest and most frequently reiterated aspects of his approach to peace. It is entirely fitting that the initial chapter of Norman Thomas' final book, *The Choices,* is entitled "We Must Choose Peace."[71] Its major thesis, his insistence that Americans must choose peace as their basic approach to the problems confronting them, symbolized the preeminent position which peace came to occupy in the reform efforts of his later years. In support of peace, he repeated in highly compressed form the plan which he had expounded in his previously discussed book, *The Prerequisites for Peace.*

The first chapter of *The Choices* is thus fitting for two reasons: it summarizes the state of a major theme in Thomas' writing at the end of his career, and it illustrates how he continued to use his writing as an integral part of his reform efforts. Throughout his life, Thomas' hopes for peace were accompanied by plans for its achievement. He ended as he had begun: challenging the world to seek alternatives to war as a means of resolving human conflict. Basic to his position were his beliefs that man did not have to accept the inevitability of war and that mankind possessed the power to create and choose alternatives. Thomas' faith explained his lifelong exposition of such beliefs and also his remark in *The Choices* that "All of these things must be based upon and supported by a general ideal of fraternity to which each nation may make its own particular contribution."[72] Humanism proved to be the ultimate weapon in Norman Thomas' struggle against war.

CHAPTER 8

The Lasting Thomas

I *Perspective on the Reformer as Writer*

NORMAN Thomas' writing presents the student of American literature with the best opportunity to examine the social activist as nonfiction writer in twentieth-century America. With the exception of a few pieces of literary criticism and a few anecdotal articles, all of his literary efforts were part of his attempt to create a more just American society in a peaceful world. While his writing has intrinsic value as an annotated index to the vast number of problems which have confronted Americans in this century, it is even more important to remember that Thomas' writing was a passionate polemic—it contains the most comprehensive advocacy of Democratic Socialist humanism found in twentieth-century American literature.

The intensity of concern and the deep sense of understanding which marked Thomas' treatment of the major issues of his lifetime are also significant. The interaction of these factors with his faith in Democratic Socialism created a definite tension in his writing similar to that found in the writing of numerous other American reformers.[1] On the one hand, his graphic portrayal of the injustices which he found in American society created a strong sense of realism in his writing. On the other hand, his faith in Democratic Socialist solutions injected a strong strain of idealism. Alden Whitman summarized the essence of Thomas' idealism in a moving obituary in the *New York Times* when he said: "His unrealized ideal was an American cooperative commonwealth, whose chief features were to be public ownership and democratic control of all the basic means of production as well as long range economic planning."[2] The contrast between what America was and what he wanted it to be was the very essence of his writing.

To dismiss most of Norman Thomas' writings as his biographer Harry Fleischman did as "tracts for the times" with little lasting value is highly questionable. Most American reform writing could be dismissed as insignificant on the same grounds. Whether taken individually or collectively, Thomas' articles and books present a remarkably well-informed exposition of the major political, economic, and social issues which Americans have faced in the twentieth century. The sense of immediacy which pervaded his writing was the inevitable product of his intense personal involvement with the events and people about whom he wrote. Certainly, Thomas wrote about current events for people who were involved in them, and his writings were indeed "tracts for the times" in that sense. However, these same "tracts" provide significant insights into such aspects of Thomas' reform personality as his love for his country, his thirst for social justice, and his hopes for a peaceful world. They present contemporary readers with an excellent example of the American reform mind at work, and they also underscore the continuity of essential elements of American radical-reform thought from Thomas Paine to Norman Thomas. Thomas' books and articles prove the persistence of his attempts to educate the generally indifferent American public about the potential of Democratic Socialism, not as a rigid ideological system, but as a way of life.

Moreover, Thomas' writing presents students of American literature and reform thought with a splendid opportunity to examine the problems encountered by the social-activist writer in contemporary American society. It provides the reader with ample opportunity to see the modern reform writer as he struggles with the demands of immediacy, the limitations and advantages of personal involvement, and the desire to persuade his generally indifferent audience of the truth of his beliefs. Thomas' writing contains numerous examples, as evidenced by his own frequent references, to the frustration which he suffered because the American people agreed with his criticisms but refused to accept his proposed solutions to the problems about which he wrote.[3]

II *The Respected Thomas*

What explains the tremendous amount of respect which

Norman Thomas commanded from his fellow Americans throughout his long life?[4] How did it happen that the man who commanded the American Socialist party during the period of its demise rose during the same period to such a highly respected and esteemed position in the eyes of his fellow Americans? Obviously, an important part of the explanation for this paradox lies in the fact that those who assess Thomas' significance solely in terms of his Socialist leadership measure him too narrowly;[5] Norman Thomas was far more than a Socialist leader to many Americans. He was the conscience of America. As Alden Whitman asserted, ". . .for almost a half-century, he was uniquely the nation's conscience for social justice and social reform. He spoke to the feelings that most Americans have about themselves: that they are a fair people; that it is somehow wrong for poverty to exist amid plenty; that it is a perversion of justice to be jailed for political reasons; that Constitutional rights should be respected regardless of race and creed."[6] Both his own writings and the judgments of those who knew him well provide evidence which supports this characterization.

A number of writers have insisted that Thomas' appeal stemmed from the fact that he was much more of a moralist than a social critic. One of the editors of *The Nation* noted that Thomas was not even mentioned in Christopher Lasch's *The New Radicalism in America, 1889–1963* or in T. B. Bottomore's *Critics of Society: Radical Thought in North America.*[7] Both Murray Seidler and Harry Fleischman, Thomas' chief biographers, also emphasized his moralistic approach to problems.[8] Drawing too sharp a distinction between Thomas' moral and social criticism, however, creates a needlessly confusing dichotomy. It should not be forgotten that, while Thomas was certainly a moral critic, he was also a tremendously well-informed student of American society. True, Thomas' Socialism was certainly much closer to the Social Gospel, as advocated by Walter Rauschenbusch and as developed in Thomas' years as a slum pastor, than to the Communism of Karl Marx; but Thomas' sure use of facts, his unerring control of details, and his sure grasp of the social and economic complexities of which he wrote greatly resembled the Muckrakers of the Progressive Era. Students of American reform thought often err when they draw rigid distinctions between moralists and social critics.[9] The sharp distinction does not stand when applied to the writings of Norman Thomas. His writing suggests that he combined the two traditions just as he combined his condemnation of the evils in American society with a consistent call for the application of humanistic, rational solutions to them.

While it is possible to quibble about whether Thomas was a moral or a social critic, there is no doubt that much of Thomas' appeal came from his lifelong application of a traditional evangelical style to his reform activities. Indeed, it is highly probable that his style caused much of the confusion over the nature of his role as a social critic. Although he lost his faith relatively early in adulthood in the formal dogmatic theology of his early Christian upbringing, he was never able to free himself from the traditions of his evangelical Protestant background. He developed a reformist style which, according to Michael Harrington, ". . .incarnated a peculiarly American and Protestant sense of social justice and personal integrity."[10] Shortly before Norman Thomas suffered the stroke which forced his retirement from public life in 1967, his old friend Roger N. Baldwin warned Thomas against exhausting himself on a campus speaking tour. To this, Thomas retorted: "I know you wouldn't, but you aren't an evangelist!"[11]

Respect for Thomas was reinforced by a number of other traits in his reform personality which were evident in his writing. The flexible, nondoctrinaire nature of Thomas' Socialism which was much closer to the native American Social Gospel and humane political liberalism of the Progressives than it was to any alien political theories helped to assure his acceptance. As the eminent historian, George Mowry, noted in his assessment of the failure of organized Socialism in America: "Probably one of the main troubles with the American Socialist party was that it was so American it couldn't be socialistic. After all, Norman Thomas was the same sort of preacher as Edward Bellamy, with much the same mission in life."[12] Thomas' Socialism was never rigid or doctrinaire; he always emphasized the broadest range of human freedom, initiative, and pragmatism.

Two other aspects of Thomas' reform personality which

were clearly evident in his writing created respect for him. The first of these was the remarkable consistency of his reform goals. Roger N. Baldwin went to the heart of this point when he noted that Thomas' ". . .ends were as clear and steady as they were to be all his life—the struggle against war, for equality of rights for all people, and against poverty and injustice."[13] Thomas' unswerving devotion to these broad humanitarian goals worked to broaden his appeal far beyond the ranks of the Socialist party. Second, Thomas always remained within the context of the American society which he criticized. He made no bones about his genuine love and affection for America and his desire to improve it. In his later years, he often urged angry young radicals ". . .to wash the flag, not burn it."[14] While Thomas proposed the sharp modification of the dominant American capitalism and the excesses which he felt it spawned, he always insisted that reforms be carried out through nonviolent resort to the legal, democratic process.

Because of his refusal to alienate himself from American society in spite of his rejection of its central economic theory, Thomas became something of a bridge between American liberalism and radicalism during his lifetime.[15] The great personal respect which he commanded certainly worked to facilitate the application of "Socialist solutions" to economic problems during the rise of the welfare state in America.

III *Thomas as Adult Educator*

Any discussion of the significance of Norman Thomas would certainly be incomplete without some consideration of his role as an adult educator. Because Thomas knew that he never had any real chance to win any of his numerous campaigns for public office, he took full advantage of the superb opportunities which they offered as educational vehicles. Unrestricted by the usual political inhibitions placed on the candidates who ran to win and freed from the time-consuming duties of public office, Thomas was able to expound on the application of ethical principles to political, social, and economic issues in a way that no candidate of the major parties ever dared do. Writing in 1953, the editor of *The Christian*

Century evaluated Thomas' role as a politician-educator in the following terms:

> Those who voted for Mr. Thomas did not do so with any idea that he might win. A Norman Thomas vote was a protest vote, and an effort to draw attention to the importance of the Norman Thomas ideas. In the first purpose, those who voted for Mr. Thomas were moderately successful. In the second, they were entirely so. . . . He won no offices; his ideas, as a glance at the Democratic and Republican platforms will show, won in both parties. We hope that both Norman Thomas and his Socialists will continue to serve the nation as adult educators. For the big parties, we expect, will go right on, gigantic business combines for the control of offices. . . .[16]

That Thomas was cut off from the responsibilities of policy-making did not make him an irresponsible critic of those persons and policies he criticized. His studies of the problems about which he wrote were always grounded on a thorough knowledge of what the leading experts in the field were saying. This knowledge and his own extremely sensitive conscience prevented him from making rash assertions. They help explain why he was never dismissed as an irrelevant crank.[17]

IV *The Impact of Thomas' Writing*

The specific impact of Norman Thomas is difficult to measure. As with many American writers, the general indications of his influence are numerous. The frequent references to Thomas as the "conscience of America" and the "great dissenter" are reflections of the love and admiration shown him in later years for his unceasing devotion to his cause. Americans, as Michael Harrington said shortly before Thomas' death, are ". . .right to treat him as one of the great practical moralists of our time, but their highest tribute would be to face up to the indictment Thomas is still making."[18] Harrington's statement provides a sensible criterion for judging the impact of Norman Thomas on his countrymen and their institutions. Have Americans actually, as Harrington argued, refused to face up to Thomas' indictment of their society? What of the success of his lifelong advocacy?

Despite the rapid decline of the Socialist party after 1933,

Thomas lived to see much of what the party advocated in its early platforms enacted into law. Such things as low-cost public housing, social security, minimum-wage legislation, civil rights acts, and medicare, though in somewhat modified form, have passed from the Socialist platform by way of the New Deal into the law of the land. These and numerous other measures are now commonly accepted as part of the socioeconomic fabric of the new American welfare state.

Moreover, Thomas' writing certainly justifies the conclusion that he accurately foresaw the emergence of the welfare state in this country. As the editor of *The New Yorker* said: "And if, when it was all added up, he had been less of a revolutionary than a kind of Socialist apostle to the middle class, it was still true that a number of revolutionary changes had taken place in his lifetime. Much of the program for social and economic reform that had been dismissed as wild-eyed Bolshevism when he first got up to preach about it was now the law of the land, and taken for granted."[19] The important point to remember here is that Norman Thomas grew in public esteem ". . .not because he moderated his 'radical' proposals as the years went by, but because so much of what he advocated became the law of the land."[20] Even though Thomas complained often about his lack of success, the country certainly moved noticeably in the direction in which he pointed.[21]

Speaking and writing as the respected voice of the American conscience throughout most of his long career, his passionate calls for human justice and freedom convinced many concerned individuals outside the ranks of the Socialist party of the need for a more humane, economically just society. Thomas, respected and trusted for his absolute honesty, certainly proved to be one of the major influences working for the emergence and acceptance of the American welfare state. It is true that much of Thomas' significance lay in his ability to foresee the direction and nature of the changes which American society would have to make. However, it should not be forgotten that ". . .the deeper explanation for them lies in the ceaselessly eloquent, profoundly passionate manner in which they were advocated over the years by Mr. Thomas."[22]

Thomas remained dissatisfied to the end of his life because of the failure of organized Socialism and the unwillingness of

Americans to implement his ultimate goals, the cooperative commonwealth and world disarmament. As he made clear in his final book, *The Choices,* written shortly before his death in 1968, he remained deeply concerned about the magnitude of the problems facing Americans as they entered the 1970's.[23] The work is also proof of his continued faith in the power of his writing as a persuasive tool.

V *Thomas and the Failure of American Radicalism*

Norman Thomas' writing suggests that he is important for a markedly different reason than those previously discussed. Thomas' reform experience stands as a touchstone which explains the failure of radicalism in America. Michael Harrington best explained this aspect of Thomas' significance when he said: "Yet, if we are to understand Thomas as a man, and much of the history of contemporary American radicalism, we must confront the fact that in part he failed. The failure lies not in the fact that Thomas never became President. Rather, it is that the impact of his leadership has been almost entirely personal, that he was not able to build an effective, organized Socialist movement. . . . Thomas strove to work out an approach that would build a bridge between his ideas and organization and the complexities of American political life. He did not succeed."[24]

Norman Thomas was well aware of this failure; indeed, his continuing discussion of the causes of the failure of organized Socialism in America constituted one of the major themes in his later writing. His assessment is particularly valuable because it is an "inside view" of the demise of organized Socialism and because it is a serious attempt to analyze the various causes for it. A comparative study of Thomas' explanation of the failure of Socialism and that presented by Carl N. Degler and other scholars substantiates the accuracy of his interpretation.[25] Thomas' writing strongly suggests—in contrast to the critical treatment of his leadership presented by Bernard K. Johnpoll in his recent volume *Pacifist's Progress: Norman Thomas and the Decline of American Socialism*—that the failure of American Socialism was caused by forces beyond the power of Thomas and the party leadership.[26] The differences between the American and the European situation were simply too great to overcome. The writings of Norman Thomas may ultimately prove of lasting value because of the light they throw on this failure.

Finally, this study leads to one inescapable conclusion. Norman Thomas' writing can best be understood as a manifestation of the American liberal reform tradition which originated in the Colonial Period and continues to the present. His Socialism, when juxtaposed to traditional Marxism, was uniquely American. His advocacy of nonviolent evolutionary development, his emphasis on religious and ethical motivation, his de-emphasis of class conflict, his faith in education as a means of social change, and the nature of his critique of capitalism all attest to this fact. His writing reminds us that Norman Thomas, like most of the leading exponents of the American liberal reform tradition, chose neither Marx nor Jesus but placed his faith in man.

Notes and References

PREFACE

1. Harry Fleischman, *Norman Thomas: A Biography* (New York, 1964), p. 300.

Chapter One

1. Edward Levinson, "Norman Thomas," *Current History and Forum,* XLV, 1 (October, 1936) 72.

2. William A. H. Birnie, "Noble Norman," *The American Magazine,* CXXX, 1 (July, 1940), 44–45 and 113–16; Claude Moore Fuess, "Norman Thomas: Socialist Crusader," *Current History and Forum,* XXXVII (October, 1932), 1-6.

3. Fleischman, pp. 21–32; Murray B. Seidler, *Norman Thomas: Respectable Rebel,* 2nd ed. (Syracuse, N.Y.; 1967), pp. 4–5: *As I See It* (New York, 1932), pp. 153–65.

4. Fleischman, p. 27; Seidler, p. 4; "Letter to the Editor," *The Saturday Review of Literature,* IX (October 29, 1932), 201.

5. Seidler, p. 5.

6. Columbia Oral History Project transcript, "Socialist Movement Project: Norman Thomas" (1967), pp. 13–14; see also Thomas' "Puritan Fathers," *The Atlantic Monthly*, CXLVIII (November, 1931), 650-55 for a description of the idealism which he obtained from his early family life.

7. Record: "Norman Thomas Reminisces" (New Rochelle, N.Y.: 1959).

8. Draft of "Man of Week" article by Thomas for *Macmillan News Review* (May, 1932), Norman Thomas Papers, Box 109.

9. Columbia Oral History Project transcript, "The Reminiscences of Norman Thomas" (1949), Part I, p. 20 (Hereafter referred to as C.O.H.).

10. Record: "Norman Thomas Reminisces;" Ted to Norman Thomas (June 16, 1907 or 1908?), Norman Thomas Papers, Box 1.

11. Fleischman, pp. 42–43; Seidler, p. 13.

12. C.O.H. (1949), Part I, pp. 47–48.

13. *A Socialist's Faith* (New York, 1951), p. x.

14. Cleveland H. Dodge to Norman Thomas (January 11, 1911) and Norman Thomas to Mr. Adriance (May 19, 1912), Norman Thomas Papers, Box 1; C.O.H. (1949), Part I, pp. 19–20.

15. Norman Thomas to Princeton classmates (December 6, 1915), Norman Thomas Papers, Box 1.

16. Norman Thomas to the Rev. Howard A. Walter (January 31, 1917), Norman Thomas Papers, Box 2; "Correspondence," *The New Republic,* XI (July 7, 1917), 274-75.

17. C.O.H. (1949), Part I, pp. 120–23.

18. "What of the Church?," *The New World,* I (February, 1918), 44; see also Norman Thomas to Dr. Laidlaw (March 15, 1917), Norman Thomas Papers, Box 2.

19. Norman Thomas to Morris Hillquit (October 2, 1917), Norman Thomas Papers, Box 3; Record: "Norman Thomas Reminisces."

20. Norman Thomas to the Rev. Frank Fitt (April 3, 1917), Norman Thomas Papers, Box 2; Fleischman, pp. 63–64.

21. Norman Thomas to Alexander Trachtenberg (October 18, 1918), Norman Thomas Papers, Box 4; see also C.O.H. (1949), Part I, pp. 20–22.

22. Record: "Norman Thomas Reminisces."

23. *Ibid.*; Fleischman, p. 59.

24. Author's interview with Maurice Goldbloom, New York City, July 29, 1970 (Hereafter referred to as Goldbloom interview.); Roger N. Baldwin, "Norman Thomas: A Combative Life," *The New Republic,* CLVIII, 2 (January 13, 1968), 11–12.

25. C.O.H. (1949), Part I, pp. 46-47; Seidler, pp. 91-96.

26. C.O.H. (1949), Part I, pp. 26-28; "Labor and the Press," *Forum,* LXXI (May, 1924), 587–96; "Norman Thomas Tells of Journalism Career," *Editor and Publisher,* LXXXVI, 3 (January 17, 1953), 55.

27. C.O.H. (1966), Part II, pp. 40–42; (with Harry Laidler, joint editors), *New Tactics of Social Conflict* (New York, 1926), pp. iii–vii; Seidler, pp. 73–74.

28. Goldbloom interview. Laidler did the research while Thomas did the speaking and writing.

29. C.O.H. (1949), Part I, pp. 80–81; "Correspondence," *The New Republic,* XXXIV (May 9, 1923), 296–97; see William E. Leuchtenburg, *The Perils of Prosperity, 1914–1932* (Chicago, Ill.; 1958) for a clear characterization of the mood of the 1920's.

30. Record: "Norman Thomas Reminisces."

31. *Ibid.*

32. C.O.H. (1949), Part I, pp. 29-57; (with Paul Blanshard), *What's the Matter with New York: A National Problem* (New York, 1932), *passim;* "The 'Unholy Union' of Prohibition and Politics," *Current History and Forum,* XXXI (October, 1929), 58–63; "Progressivism at St. Louis," *The Nation,* CXVIII (February 27, 1924), 224–25.

33. Record: "Norman Thomas Reminisces;" *Current Biography Yearbook* (New York, 1962), p. 417.

34. *What's the Matter with New York, passim; As I See It,* pp. 113–40;

The Choice Before Us: Mankind at the Crossroads (New York, 1934), pp. 83–127; *Socialism on the Defensive* (New York, 1938), pp. 254–93; *Socialism Re-examined* (New York, 1963), pp. 117–30; *The Choices* (New York, 1969), pp. 62–81.

35. Benjamin Stolberg, "The Reading of the Candidates," *The Bookman,* LXVIII (October, 1928), 148.

36. *Ibid.*

37. "The Fate of a Gamblers' Civilization," *Current History and Forum,* XXXVI (May, 1932), 155–60; see John Kenneth Galbraith, *The Great Crash: 1929* (Boston, Mass.; 1961) for a discussion of its causes and effects.

38. Norman Thomas to Franklin D. Roosevelt (January 20, 1932), Norman Thomas Papers, Box 5; Record: "Norman Thomas Reminisces;" "Socialism Upheld," *The World Tomorrow,* XIII (February, 1930), 70–73; *America's Way Out: A Program for Democracy* (New York, 1931), *passim.*

39. "Letter to the Editor," p. 201.

40. *America's Way Out, passim: As I See It, passim; The Choice Before Us, passim;* "Socialism: The Way Out for America," *The World Tomorrow,* XIV (March, 1931), 72–74.

41. Thomas' article "The Fate of a Gamblers' Civilization," pp. 155–60 is perhaps his most cogent exposition of this idea.

42. Norman Thomas to Amicus Most (October 5, 1933) and Norman Thomas to Clarence Senior (November 14, 1933), Norman Thomas Papers, Box 6; C.O.H. (1949), Part I, pp. 65–74.

43. Levinson, "Norman Thomas," pp. 74–75.

44. C.O.H. (1949), Part I, p. 63; C.O.H. (1966), Part II, pp. 83–89; *Current Biography Yearbook,* p. 418.

45. C.O.H. (1966), Part II, pp. 85–89; Fleischman, pp. 169–70.

46. Record: "Norman Thomas Reminisces."

47. *Ibid.*; Fleischman, p. 183; Leuchtenburg, p. 188.

48. "Surveying the New Deal," *The World Tomorrow,* XVII (January 18, 1934), 38; "The New Deal: No Program of Security," *The Southern Review,* I (1935), 365–72.

49. *Ibid.*; *The Choice Before Us,* pp. 83–127.

50. Record: "Norman Thomas Reminisces."

51. *Ibid.*; H. L. Mitchell to Norman Thomas (November 7, 1933), Norman Thomas Papers, Box 6; M. S. Venkataramani, "Norman Thomas, Arkansas Sharecroppers, and the Roosevelt Agricultural Policies, 1933–1937," *The Mississippi Valley Historical Review,* XLVII (September, 1960), 225–46.

52. Fleischman, pp. 155–56.

53. Record: "Norman Thomas Reminisces;" "Hoosier Hitlerism," *The Nation,* CXLI (September 18, 1935), 324–26.

54. *Human Exploitation in the United States* (New York, 1934), *passim.*
55. *Ibid.,* p. 388.
56. C.O.H. (1966), Part II, pp. 74–83; "Bolshevism, Violence and Expropriation," *The World Tomorrow,* II (March, 1919), 79–80; see also Philip Foner, ed., *The Bolshevik Revolution: Its Impact on American Radicals, Liberals, and Labor* (New York, 1967), *passim;* Sidney Lens, *Radicalism in America* (New York, 1966), pp. 257–58.
57. "Reflections on Russia and Revolution," *The World Tomorrow,* III (September, 1920), 259–62.
58. C.O.H. (1949), Part I, p. 61; Fleischman, p. 189.
59. C.O.H. (1949), Part I, pp. 109–11; Fleischman, p. 168.
60. Record: "Norman Thomas Reminisces;" *The Choice Before Us,* pp. 151–52.
61. Draft of statement for Socialist party on Moscow Purge Trials (1936), Norman Thomas Papers, Box 109.
62. Record: "Norman Thomas Reminisces."
63. *As I See It,* pp. 23 and 100; *Human Exploitation,* p. 388.
64. "The Pacifist's Dilemma," *The Nation,* CXLIV (January 16, 1937), 66–68.
65. C.O.H. (1966), Part II, p. 140; see also Thomas' "Spain: A Socialist View," *The Nation,* CXLIV (June 19, 1937), 698–700.
66. C.O.H. (1966), Part II, pp. 140–41. The last chapter of Thomas' book, *A Socialist's Faith,* contains an excellent assessment of his work for peace from 1935–41.
67. Record: "Norman Thomas Reminisces;" "How Can We Escape War?," *The Nation,* CXLV (December 25, 1937), 707–09; "Collective Security and Socialism," *Socialist Review,* VI, 6 (May-June, 1938), 4–5 and 15.
68. "How to Fight for Democracy," *The Annals of the American Academy of Political and Social Science,* CCXVI (July, 1941), 58–64.
69. *A Socialist's Faith,* pp. 313–14; see also C.O.H. (1966), Part II, pp. 140–41.
70. "Letters to the Editors," *The Nation,* CLIV (January 31, 1942), 124.
71. *World Federation: What Are the Difficulties?* (New York, 1942), *passim; What Is Our Destiny?* (Garden City, N.Y.; 1944), *passim.*
72. "Totalitarian Liberals," *The Commonweal,* XXXVII (January 22, 1943), 342.
73. "Dark Day for Liberty," *The Christian Century,* LIX (July 29, 1942), 929–31; Fleischman, p. 205.
74. Record: "Norman Thomas Reminisces;" Fleischman, pp. 210-11.
75. Record: "Norman Thomas Reminisces."
76. Lens, pp. 362-64; Michael Harrington, *Toward a New Democratic Left: A Radical Program for a New Majority* (Baltimore, Md.; 1968),

passim; Harry W. Laidler, *History of Socialism* (New York, 1968), pp. 819–20.

77. "Arming Against Russia," *The Annals of the American Academy of Political and Social Science,* CCXLI (September, 1945), 67–71; "What Shall We Do for Peace?," *The Christian Century,* LXIV (September 24, 1947), 1137–38.

78. Fleischman, p. 252; see Eric F. Goldman, *The Crucial Decade: America, 1945–1955* (New York, 1959) for a description of the impact of the Cold War on American society.

79. Norman Thomas to M. E. Edson (December 20, 1932), Norman Thomas Papers, Box 5; C.O.H. (1966), Part II, pp. 93–100.

80. *A Socialist's Faith,* p. x.

81. "Our One Hope for Peace," *The Saturday Evening Post,* CCXXIV, 31 (February 2, 1952), 25 and 75–76; Dwight MacDonald, "Politics," *Esquire,* LXVII, 3 (March, 1967), 30, 32, and 34–35.

82. MacDonald, "Politics," pp. 34–35.

83. C.O.H. (1966), Part II, p. 106.

84. *A Socialist's Faith, passim; Socialism Re-examined, passim; The Choices, passim;* "Rethinking Socialism," *The Virginia Quarterly Review,* XXXIV (Winter, 1958), 43–54.

85. Letter to author from Professor Henry Pelling, Oxford University (May 1, 1970).

86. Fleischman, pp. 238–49; Seidler, pp. 233–37.

87. Seidler, pp. 236–37; "Appraisal of Political Parties," *Vital Speeches of the Day,* XIV (October 1, 1948), 746–49.

88. "Rethinking Socialism," pp. 43–54; "I'm Glad I'm Not Running This Time!," *American Magazine,* CLIV, 4 (October, 1952), 19 and 100–03; Laidler, pp. 817–19.

89. See, for example, "A Socialist Reports on Socialism," *The New York Times Magazine* (October 30, 1955), pp. 15, 38, 42, and 47.

90. "The Failure of Organized Socialism in America," *The Progressive,* XXIII, 1 (January, 1959), 29–32; Fleischman, pp. 238–49; Seidler, pp. 303–14.

91. Harold E. Fey, review of *Norman Thomas: A Biography* by Harry Fleischman, *The Christian Century,* LXXXI (July 22, 1964), 938.

92. Record: "Norman Thomas Reminisces;" Fleischman, pp. 210–11.

93. "Civil Rights—But Not Conspiracy," *The New York Times Magazine* (January 7, 1951), pp. 11, 41–42, and 44; *The Test of Freedom* (New York, 1954), *passim.*

94. See, for example, Thomas' eloquent statement before Congress on the Civil Rights Bill of 1964 in "Should Congress Enact the Employment Nondiscrimination Provisions of the Civil Rights Bill?," *Congressional Digest,* XLIII (March, 1964), 92 and 94.

95. *The Choices,* pp. 9–24.

96. Record: "Norman Thomas Reminisces."

97. Seidler, p. 319; *The Prerequisites for Peace* (New York, 1959), *passim; The Choices,* pp. 1–8.

98. "A Message to Johnson," *Sane World,* V, 1 (January, 1966), 2.

99. Record: "Norman Thomas Reminisces;" *Appeal to the Nations* (New York, 1947), *passim; The Prerequisites for Peace, passim; The Choices,* pp. 1-8; "Our One Hope for Peace," pp. 25 and 75-76.

100. "Are We As Right As We Think?," *Saturday Review,* XLII (April 18, 1959), 13.

101. *The Choice Before Us,* p. 158; *Socialism Re-examined,* pp. 113-14; Seidler, p. 317. Thomas, himself, regarded the Socialism which he espoused as a significant addition and modification of the earlier native tradition. Murray B. Seidler prefers to argue somewhat more generally that Thomas was in the radical-liberal democratic tradition.

102. Lens, pp. 1–4.

103. Fleischman, pp. 307–08; see Thomas' essay on Wendell Phillips in *Great Dissenters* (New York, 1961), pp. 129–68; Richard Hofstadter, *The Age of Reform: From Bryan to F. D. R.* (New York, 1955), pp. 131–214.

104. "The Dissenter's Role in a Totalitarian Age," *The New York Times Magazine* (November 20, 1949), p. 78; see Thomas' book, *Great Dissenters,* for insight into his beliefs regarding the nature and uses of dissent.

105. C.O.H. (1966), Part II, p. 73.

106. Goldbloom interview; C.O.H. (1949 and 1966), Part I and II, *passim; The Choice Before Us,* pp. 63–82; *Socialism on the Defensive,* pp. 105–64 and 233–53; *Socialism Re-examined,* pp. 32–63.

107. "Socialism's Impact on America," *Modern Review,* II (January, 1948), 23.

108. See footnote #106 in this chapter.

109. See, for example, articles on the failure of American Socialism such as Thomas' "The Failure of Organized Socialism in America," pp. 29–32.

Chapter Two

1. *Mr. Chairman, Ladies, and Gentlemen: Reflections of Public Speaking* (New York, 1955), *passim;* "Random Reflections on Public Speaking," *The Quarterly Journal of Speech,* XL (April, 1954), 145–51.

2. Goldbloom interview.

3. *The Conscientious Objector in America* (New York, 1923) reissued as *Is Conscience a Crime?* (New York, 1927), p. vii.

4. *America's Way Out,* p. viii.

5. Goldbloom interview. Mr. Goldbloom suggested that this habit was a carryover from Thomas' ministerial career and that he found it

to be a convenient means of presenting material throughout his lifetime.

6. "What of the Church?," pp. 44–45; *A Socialist's Faith,* p. 139 and *passim.*

7. Goldbloom interview.

8. *The Test of Freedom,* p. vii; Goldbloom interview. Mr. Goldbloom insisted that Thomas did no formal research for most of his books and articles beyond his habitual intensive reading in American economics, politics, and sociology.

9. *Socialism Re-examined,* pp. 7–9.

10. *As I See It,* Preface; Goldbloom interview.

11. *As I See It,* Preface; *Great Dissenters,* p. 18.

12. Research under a grant provided by the National Endowment for the Humanities, summer of 1970, indicates Thomas was cognizant of European Socialist affairs and activities of the Second International but never to the extent that Morris Hillquit was. There was no continuing correspondence between Thomas and the members of the Second International as there was between Hillquit and Friedrich Alder. Hillquit-Alder correspondence, International Institute of Social History, Amsterdam (June 28, 1923–June 12, 1931), Box 2893. Thomas' opposition to American involvement in European affairs in the years preceding World War II aroused much opposition among the leaders of the Second International and worked to lessen his contacts with European Socialists. Author's translation of a letter from Friedrich Adler to Marmorek (February 17, 1941), provided by Dr. Wanda Lanzer, Society for Labor History, Vienna.

13. Fleischman, p. 301. Outstanding examples of this combination of experience and reading can be found throughout Thomas' writing. See, for example, his *Is Conscience a Crime?* and *Human Exploitation* for earlier manifestations of this trait and his *Socialism Re-examined* and *The Choices* for later ones.

14. "Correspondence," *The New Republic* (July 7, 1917), pp. 274–75. Thomas' article "Random Reflections on Public Speaking," pp. 145–51 substantiates his emphasis on sincerity in his persuasive activities.

15. Goldbloom interview. Mr. Goldbloom pointed out the basic evangelical similiarities of the Social Gospel and Democratic Socialism.

16. C.O.H. (1949), Part I, pp. 22–25.

17. *A Socialist's Faith,* pp. 306–07. Especially good examples of this aspect can be found in the concluding chapters of most of Thomas' books and the final paragraphs of many of his articles.

18. *The Choice Before Us,* pp. 234-35; see also *A Socialist's Faith,* p. 118; *What Is Our Destiny?,* p. 5; *The Choices,* p. viii.

19. *Human Exploitation,* pp. 388–89.

20. *Is Conscience a Crime?*, p. 5; see also *The Choice Before Us*, p. 190.
21. *The Test of Freedom*, p. 193.
22. Stolberg, "The Reading of the Candidates," p. 148.
23. "Eugene Victor Debs," *Current History and Forum*, XXV (December, 1926), 375–76; see also "Correspondence," *The Nation*, CXXVII (September 5, 1928), 226–27; "Mr. Wilson's Tragedy and Ours," *The World Tomorrow*, IV (March, 1921), 81–84.
24. *Great Dissenters, passim.*
25. *A Socialist's Faith*, p. 101; see also "Great Challenge of the Dissenter," *The New York Times Magazine* (November 5, 1959), p. 56.
26. "Twisting Tammany's Tail," *Forum*, LXXXV (June, 1931), 335; "What Has Roosevelt Accomplished?," *The Nation*, CXXXVI (April 12, 1933), 399–400; "The Fate of a Gamblers' Civilization," pp. 155–60; *The Test of Freedom*, p. 192.
27. "Organization or Violence?," *The Nation*, CIX (October 4, 1919), 461.
28. "Seeing the World with the Marines," *The World Tomorrow*, IX (November, 1926), 195–96.
29. "Appraisal of Political Parties," pp. 746–49.
30. *As I See It*, pp. 162–63; see also *A Socialist's Faith*, p. 268.
31. Norman Thomas, review of *The Passing of Normalcy* by Charles W. Wood, *The Saturday Review of Literature*, VI (February 1, 1930), 689–90; Norman Thomas, review of *Business and the Public Interests* by Benjamin Javits, *The Twelfth Hour of Capitalism* by Keno Renatus and *Is Capitalism Doomed?* by Lawrence Dennis, *The World Tomorrow*, XV (June, 1932), 186–87; Norman Thomas, review of *On Our Way* by Franklin D. Roosevelt, *The Saturday Review of Literature*, X (April 14, 1934), 625–26; Norman Thomas, review of *Three Who Made a Revolution: A Biographical History* by Bertram D. Wolfe and *Stalin and German Communism, A Study in the Origins of the State Party* by Ruth Fischer, *The American Mercury*, LXVIII (February, 1949), 236–43.
32. "Some Wrong Roads to Peace," *Vital Speeches of the Day*, XI (September 14, 1943), 721; *As I See It*, p. 77; "A Socialist Looks at the Constitution," *The Annals of the American Academy of Political and Social Science*, CLXXXV (May, 1936), 93.
33. "The Pacifist's Dilemma," p. 67.
34. *As I See It*, pp. 146–47.
35. *The Choice Before Us*, p. 198.
36. *Ibid.*, p. 61; *Socialism Re-examined*, p. 73.
37. Consider, for example, the writings of Earl Browder and William Foster of the American Communist party and Morris Hillquit and Eugene V. Debs of the American Socialist party.
38. "I'm Glad I'm Not Running This Time!," p. 19.
39. "Puritan Fathers," p. 652.

Chapter Three

1. Norman Thomas Papers, Box 1, *passim.*
2. Norman Thomas to Jack (March 30, 1917), Norman Thomas Papers, Box 2; *A Socialist's Faith,* p. 6.
3. *New Tactics in Social Conflict,* p. vii.
4. "Socialism Upheld," p. 70; see also *As I See It,* p. 25.
5. By the time Thomas had lived through the 1950's, he was convinced that capitalism was a lot more durable than he had thought earlier in his career. See Chapter 4, footnote #41.
6. *Human Exploitation,* p. 384; see also "Why I Am a Socialist," *Independent Woman,* XIII (October, 1934), 332–33.
7. *As I See It,* p. 26, see also p. 42; "Socialism Upheld," p. 70.
8. *As I See It,* p. 388.
9. Norman Thomas, review of *The Passing of Normalcy,* p. 690.
10. *America's Way Out,* p. 22; see also "A Socialist Looks at the Swope Plan," *The Nation,* CXXXIII (October 7, 1931), 359.
11. "Capitalism Will Not Plan," *The New Republic,* LXVII (August 12, 1931), 339.
12. *As I See It,* p. 27; *The Choice Before Us,* p. 22.
13. "Socialism Upheld," p. 71.
14. *Human Exploitation,* p. 383; *The Choices,* p. 29.
15. "The Fate of a Gamblers' Civilization," p. 158.
16. *New Tactics in Social Conflict,* p. 155.
17. *The Choice Before Us,* pp. 25–26.
18. *Ibid.,* p. 29.
19. *Ibid.,* p. 62.
20. "Labor's Greatness—And Some Weaknesses," *The World Tomorrow,* VIII (January, 1925), 8; *As I See It,* p. 27.
21. "Organization or Violence?," p. 46; see also "Labor's Greatness—And Some Weaknesses," pp. 8–10.
22. "Correspondence," *The World Tomorrow,* XV (August, 1932), 239.
23. "The Status of Radicalism in America," *The World Tomorrow,* IV (December, 1921), 370.
24. "Socialism Upheld," pp. 70–73; "The World As I Want It," *Forum,* XCII (October, 1934), 235; "Vote Socialist!," *The Christian Century,* LIII (September 30, 1936), 1283–84.
25. *As I See It,* pp. 23 and 100; *Human Exploitation,* p. 388.
26. *As I See It,* p. 99.
27. *Ibid.,* see also "The World As I Want It," p. 235.
28. *As I See It,* p. 103.
29. "Proposals for Action at Detroit," pp. 206–08; "The Marxists Reply to Corey," *The Nation,* CL (March 9, 1940), 328–29; "Fight Fascism," essay in Socialist party convention program (1934), pp. 4 and

49; "Why I Am a Socialist," pp. 332-33; *The Choice Before Us,* pp. 7 and 42-62. Thomas devoted his entire book, *Socialism on the Defensive,* to the problems posed by Fascism.

30. "Toward the American Commonwealth," *The Social Frontier,* IV (January, 1938), 128.

31. "Socialism Upheld," p. 70.

32. "Correspondence," *The World Tomorrow* (August, 1932), p. 239; see also *The Choice Before Us,* p. 145.

33. "Correspondence," *The World Tomorrow* (August, 1932), p. 239.

34. See *The Choice Before Us* and *The Choices* as examples.

35. "Our Changing Ways of Living," *Scribner's Magazine,* LXXXIX (January, 1931), 77.

36. C.O.H. (1966), Part II, pp. 40–42; see Thomas' "Youth and the American Colleges," *The Nation,* CXVII (August 1, 1923), 106–07 regarding the problems which he encountered while working with college youth.

37. "Correspondence," *The New Republic* (May 9, 1923), p. 296.

38. *Ibid.*

39. *Ibid.*

40. *Ibid.*

41. *Ibid.,* pp. 296–97.

42. *Ibid.,* p. 297.

43. *Ibid.*

44. "Toward the American Commonwealth," pp. 127–31.

45. "Collective Security and Socialism," p. 15.

Chapter Four

1. "Socialism Upheld," p. 72; see also "Our Immediate Task," *The World Tomorrow,* XVII (February 15, 1934), 83–84; *The Choice Before Us,* pp. 70–73 and 233.

2. "Socialism Upheld," p. 72.

3. See, for example, "Socialism: The Way Out for America," pp. 72–74; "Our Immediate Task," pp. 83–84.

4. *America's Way Out,* p. vii.

5. *Ibid.*

6. See Chapter 3, Section II.

7. "Capitalism Will Not Plan," p. 339; see also "Socialism: The Way Out for America," pp. 72–74; *Human Exploitation,* p. 387.

8. *As I See It,* p. 91; *Human Exploitation,* p. 386; "A Socialist Looks at the Swope Plan," pp. 357–59.

9. "A Socialist Looks at the Swope Plan," p. 359; see also *As I See It,* p. 91.

10. *As I See It,* pp. 91–92.

11. *Ibid.,* p. 92.

12. *Ibid.,* pp. 95–96.
13. "Socialism Upheld," pp. 72–73.
14. *Ibid.;* see also similar statements in "Socialism: The Way Out for America," pp. 72–74; *Human Exploitation,* p. 388, *America's Way Out,* p. vii.
15. "Socialism Upheld," p. 73.
16. *The Choice Before Us,* p. 233.
17. "Labor's Greatness—And Some Weaknesses," pp. 8-10.
18. *Ibid.,* p. 9.
19. *Ibid.,* p. 10.
20. *Ibid.*
21. *Ibid.*
22. Thomas' dream did not die easily. His writing in the 1930's, though less optimistic, still reflects his hope for organized labor. See, for example, *The Choice Before Us,* p. 232.
23. *The Choices,* pp. 39–42.
24. "Reader's Forum," *Cooperation,* XVIII (October, 1932), 197; see also "Cooperative Stores vs. Chain Stores," *Cooperation,* XVIII (July, 1932), 137-38.
25. "Vote Socialist!," pp. 1283–84.
26. "Socialism Upheld," p. 73.
27. "American Socialism's Weakest Link," *The World Tomorrow,* XVII (April 12, 1934), 182.
28. See *International Information,* XIII (June 20, 1936), 235–37 for a summation of the "Old Guard"-"Militant" controversy.
29. "Why Not a New Party?," *North American Review,* CCXXVII (February, 1929), 143–50; "American Socialism's Weakest Link," pp. 180–82; "Letters to the Editors," *The Nation,* CXLIX (October 28, 1939), 479; see also Thomas' 1963 book, *Socialism Re-examined, passim.*
30. "Correspondence," *The World Tomorrow,* XII (September, 1929), 379–80; "Socialism Upheld," pp. 70–73; "Our Changing Ways of Living," pp. 73–77.
31. "The World As I Want It," p. 235.
32. *Ibid.*
33. *Ibid.*
34. "Credo of an Old-Fashioned Socialist," *The American Mercury,* LVI (April, 1943), 464.
35. *Ibid.*
36. *Ibid.,* p. 465.
37. *Ibid.*
38. *Ibid.,* p. 466.
39. *Ibid.,* pp. 466–67.
40. *Ibid.,* p. 469.
41. *A Socialist's Faith,* pp. 4 and 33; see also "A Socialist Reports on Socialism," pp. 15, 38, 42, and 47; "Rethinking Socialism," pp. 43–54;

"The Failure of Organized Socialism in America," pp. 29–32.

42. *Socialism Re-examined,* p. 114.

43. *Ibid.,* pp. 116-17; see also "The Failure of Organized Socialism in America," p. 30.

44. *Socialism Re-examined,* p. 120.

45. "Rethinking Socialism," pp. 47–48.

46. *Ibid.,* p. 52.

47. *Socialism Re-examined,* pp. 130–34; "A Socialist Reports on Socialism," pp. 15, 38, 42, and 47.

48. *Socialism Re-examined,* p. 112.

49. *Ibid.,* p. 130.

50. *Ibid.,* p. 129–30.

51. A clear earlier statement of this hope appeared in "A Socialist Reports on Socialism," p. 47.

52. *Socialism Re-examined,* p. 208.

53. *Ibid.,* p. 209.

Chapter Five

1. *Is Conscience a Crime?,* p. 55; see also Chapter 1, footnotes #16 and 17.

2. "A Communication," *The New Republic,* XI (May 26, 1917), 109–11; see also "Correspondence," *The New Republic* (July 7, 1917), pp. 274–75; "Letters," *The Nation,* CV (August 23, 1917), 198–99.

3. "A Communication," p. 109.

4. *Ibid.*

5. *Ibid.,* p. 110.

6. *Ibid.*

7. *Ibid.*

8. See Chapter 2, footnote #3.

9. *Is Conscience a Crime?,* Dedication.

10. *Ibid.,* p. vii.

11. *Ibid.,* p. ix.

12. *Ibid.,* p. 251.

13. *Ibid.,* p. 7.

14. *Ibid.,* p. 9.

15. *Ibid.,* pp. 9–10.

16. *Ibid.,* see, for example, pp. 11, 167, 264, and 273.

17. See, for example, "Correspondence," *The New Republic,* XXXII (October 25, 1922) 222–23.

18. *Is Conscience a Crime?,* p. 30.

19. *Ibid.,* p. 55.

20. *Ibid.,* p. 264.

21. *Ibid.,* pp. 266–67.

22. *Ibid.,* p. 273.

23. *Ibid.*, p. 260.
24. Lens, pp. 248–51.
25. "A Visit to Tom Mooney," *The Nation,* CXXVII (October 24, 1928), 423–24.
26. *Ibid.*
27. *Ibid.*, p. 424.
28. *Ibid.*
29. *Ibid.*
30. *Ibid.*
31. *Ibid.*
32. *Ibid.*
33. Norman Thomas, review of *Liberty* by Everett Dean Martin, *The Saturday Review of Literature,* VI (June 7, 1930), 1101–04.
34. *Ibid.*, p. 1102.
35. *Ibid.*
36. *Ibid.*
37. *Ibid.*, p. 1103.
38. *Ibid.*
39. *Ibid.*
40. *Ibid.*
41. *Ibid.*, p. 1104.
42. " 'Hire Learning' at Ohio State, *The Nation,* CXXXII (June 17, 1931), 654–56.
43. *Ibid.*, p. 654.
44. *Ibid.*, p. 656.
45. *Ibid.*
46. *Ibid.*
47. *Ibid.*
48. *Ibid.*
49. "Can Our Schools Face Facts?," *Progressive Education,* IX (May, 1932), 338–40.
50. *Ibid.*, p. 338.
51. *Ibid.*, see also Alvin Toffler, *Future Shock* (New York, 1970).
52. "Can Our Schools Face Facts?," p. 338. Thomas repeated his call for the teaching of controversial issues in "The School at the Crossroads," *The Journal of Health and Physical Education,* VI, 2 (February, 1935), 5-6 and 61.
53. "Hoosier Hitlerism," pp. 324–26.
54. *Ibid.*, p. 324.
55. *Ibid.*
56. *Ibid.*, pp. 324–25.
57. *Ibid.*, pp. 325–26.
58. *Ibid.*, p. 326.
59. "Dark Day for Liberty," pp. 929–31; see also Norman Thomas' review of *Minorities of Oriental Race in Canada* by Canadian Institute

of International Affairs, *The Japanese in Hawaii Under War Conditions* by Andrew W. Lind, and *Japanese Evacuation: Interim Report* by Carey McWilliams, *Pacific Affairs,* XVI (March, 1943), 92-95.

60. "Dark Day for Liberty," p. 929.
61. *Ibid.*
62. *Ibid.*
63. *Ibid.*
64. *Ibid.*
65. *Ibid.*
66. *Ibid.*
67. *Ibid.,* p. 931.

Chapter Six

1. Goldman, *passim.*
2. "Civil Rights—But Not Conspiracy," pp. 11, 41–42, and 44.
3. *Ibid.,* p. 11.
4. *Ibid.*
5. *Ibid.,* p. 41.
6. *Ibid.*
7. *Ibid.*
8. *Ibid.*
9. *Ibid.*
10. *Ibid.,* p. 42.
11. *Ibid.*
12. *Ibid.*
13. *Ibid.,* p. 44.
14. *Ibid.*
15. *Ibid.*
16. *Ibid.*
17. *Ibid.*
18. *The Test of Freedom,* p. 196.
19. *Ibid.,* p. 197.
20. See David Reisman, *Lonely Crowd: A Study of the Changing American Character* (New Haven, Conn.; 1950) and Vance Packard, *The Status Seekers* (New York, 1959) for discussions of conformity in post-war American life. See Thomas' "The 'Isms' Are Out," *The Reporter,* XII, 4 (February 24, 1955), 33–34 for a discussion of conformity and the corporate mentality.
21. *Great Dissenters, passim.*
22. "The Dissenter's Role in a Totalitarian Age," pp. 13, 76, and 78–79; see also "Great Challenge of the Dissenter," pp. 24, 54, 56, 59, 62, and 64.
23. "The Dissenter's Role in a Totalitarian Age," p. 13.
24. *Ibid.*

25. *Ibid.*
26. *Ibid.*
27. *Ibid.*, p. 76.
28. *Ibid.*
29. *Ibid.*, p. 78.
30. *Ibid.*
31. *Great Dissenters,* p. 11; see also "Great Challenge of the Dissenter," p. 24.
32. *Great Dissenters,* p. 13.
33. *Ibid.*, p. 11.
34. *Ibid.*, p. 17.
35. *Ibid.*
36. Norman Thomas to Dwight D. Eisenhower (September 6, 1956), Eisenhower Papers, Eisenhower Presidential Library, Abilene, Kansas, Box 916, General File.
37. Norman Thomas to Maxwell M. Rabb, *ibid.*
38. Norman Thomas to Dwight D. Eisenhower, *Ibid.*
39. *Ibid.*
40. *Ibid.*
41. *Ibid.*
42. *Ibid.*
43. "Should Congress Enact the Employment Nondiscrimination Provisions of the Civil Rights Bill?," pp. 92 and 94.
44. *Ibid.*, p. 92.
45. *Ibid.*
46. *Ibid.*
47. *Ibid.;* see *The Choices,* pp. 9–24 for a discussion of Thomas' increasing concern about racial polarization in American life.
48. "Should Congress Enact the Employment Nondiscrimination Provisions of the Civil Rights Bill?," p. 94.
49. *The Choices,* pp. 47–56.
50. *Ibid.*, p. 47.
51. *Ibid.*, p. 48.
52. *Ibid.*, p. 49.
53. *Ibid.*, p. 48.
54. *Ibid.*, p. 49.
55. *Ibid.*
56. *Ibid.*, p. 53.
57. *Ibid.*, p. 55.

Chapter Seven

1. *A Socialist's Faith,* pp. 308–21.
2. *Ibid.*, p. 308.
3. "Is Violence the Way?," *The World Tomorrow,* II (May, 1919), 117–20.

4. *Ibid.*, p. 117.
5. *Ibid.*
6. *Ibid.*
7. *Ibid.*, p. 118.
8. *Ibid.*
9. *Ibid.*
10. *Ibid.*
11. *Ibid.*, p. 119.
12. *Ibid.*
13. *Ibid.*, p. 120.
14. *Ibid.*
15. "The Outlawry of War," *The World Tomorrow,* VII (January, 1924), 9–11.
16. Robert H. Ferrell, *American Diplomacy: A History* (New York, 1959), pp. 320–42.
17. "The Outlawry of War," p. 11.
18. *Ibid.*
19. *Ibid.*
20. *Ibid.*
21. *Ibid.*
22. *The Choice Before Us,* pp. 160-61; "Can Pacifism Act Against Injustice?," *The World Tomorrow,* VII (July, 1924), 210–12; "Recent Gains in the Quest for Peace," *The World Tomorrow,* XI (January, 1928), 8–12; "What About the Use of Violence?," *The World Tomorrow,* XV (April, 1932), 105–06; Norman Thomas, review of *Moral Man and Immoral Society* by Reinhold Niebuhr, *The World Tomorrow,* XV (December 14, 1932), 565–67; "If War Is to Be Averted" *The World Tomorrow,* XVI (October 26, 1933), 585–86.
23. *A Socialist's Faith,* p. 309.
24. *Ibid.*
25. "The Pacifist's Dilemma," pp. 66–68.
26. *Ibid.*, p. 66.
27. *Ibid.*
28. *Ibid.*
29. *Ibid.*
30. *Ibid.*, p. 67.
31. *Ibid.*
32. *Ibid.*
33. *Ibid.*
34. *Ibid.*, p. 68.
35. *Ibid.*
36. *Ibid.*
37. *Socialism on the Defensive,* pp. ix–xiii.
38. *Ibid.*, p. xii.
39. *Ibid.*, p. xiii.

40. Author's translation of a letter from Friedrich Adler to Marmorek (February 17, 1941).
41. *A Socialist's Faith,* p. 315.
42. *World Federation, passim.*
43. *Ibid.,* pp. 4–5.
44. *Ibid.,* p. 5.
45. *Ibid.,* p. 7.
46. *Ibid.,* pp. 8-9.
47. *Ibid.,* p. 9.
48. *Ibid.,* p. 12.
49. *Ibid.*
50. *Ibid.,* p. 13.
51. *Ibid.,* p. 14.
52. *Ibid.*
53. *Ibid.,* pp. 19–20.
54. *Ibid.,* p. 20.
55. *Ibid.,* p. 21.
56. *Ibid.,* p. 22.
57. *What Is Our Destiny?,* p. 88 and *passim;* "Something Better Than Dumbarton Oaks," *Vital Speeches of the Day,* XI (April 15, 1945), 402–03; "Our War with Japan," *The Commonweal,* XLII (April 20, 1945), 7–10.
58. *A Socialist's Faith,* p. 319.
59. Record: "Norman Thomas Reminisces."
60. *The Prerequisites for Peace,* p. 13.
61. *Ibid.,* pp. 26–27.
62. *Ibid.,* pp. 31–44.
63. *Ibid.,* pp. 45–57.
64. *Ibid.,* p. 58.
65. *Ibid.,* p. 64.
66. *Ibid.,* p. 89.
67. Grenville Clark and Louis Sohn, *World Peace Through Law* (Cambridge, Mass.; 1958).
68. *The Prerequisites for Peace,* pp. 158–59.
69. *Ibid.,* p. 181.
70. *Ibid.,* p. 184.
71. *The Choices,* pp. 1-8; see also "Pacifism in America," *Playboy,* XV, 12 (December, 1968), 155 and 278–83.
72. *The Choices,* p. 8.

Chapter Eight

1. See, for example, James C. Duram, "Upton Sinclair's Realistic Romanticism," *Wichita State University Studies,* XLVI (May, 1970), 1–11; Henry Steele Commager, *The American Mind* (New Haven,

Conn.; 1950), pp. 247–76; Vernon L. Parrington, *The Beginnings of Critical Realism in America, 1860–1920,* Vol. III of *Main Currents in American Thought* (New York, 1930), pp. 140–47, 301–15, and 401–15. These references do not contain specific discussions of Romantic-Realistic tension *per se,* but they do point up the awareness and concern of many American writers about the differences between American realities and ideals.

2. Alden Whitman, "The Great Reformer, Unsatisfied to the End," *New York Times* (December 22, 1968), p. 2E.

3. "If War Is to Be Averted," p. 586; "*Reflections of an Old Campaigner,*" *The Commonweal,* XLI (December 22, 1944), 246.

4. Halford E. Luccock, "Correspondence," *The Christian Century,* LXXVI (December 23, 1959), 1495.

5. David McReynolds, review of *Norman Thomas: Respectable Rebel* by Murray B. Seidler, *The Christian Century,* LXXIX (June 27, 1962), 811.

6. Whitman, p. 2E; see also Fleischman, pp. 298–309; Seidler, pp. 318–42.

7. "Norman Thomas," *The Nation,* CCVII (January 6, 1969), 5–6.

8. Fleischman, pp. 291–97 and *passim;* Seidler, pp. 253–58 and *passim;* Goldbloom interview.

9. For illustrations of the manner in which the Muckrakers merged moral and social criticisms in their works, see Arthur and Lila Weinberg, eds., *The Muckrakers* (New York, 1961).

10. Michael Harrington, review of *Norman Thomas: Respectable Rebel* by Murray B. Seidler and *Great Dissenters* by Norman Thomas, *The Reporter,* XXV (November 9, 1961), 64; see also Thomas' *As I See It,* pp. 153–65 and "Puritan Fathers," pp. 650–55 for statements of his respect for the values in the evangelical tradition which he could no longer accept.

11. Baldwin, "Norman Thomas: A Combative Life," p. 11.

12. John A. Garraty, ed., *Interpreting American History: Conversations with Historians* (London, 1970), Part II, p. 103.

13. Roger N. Baldwin, "Norman Thomas: A Memoir," *Saturday Review,* LII (April 12, 1969), 41.

14. "With Affection and Confidence," *Life,* LXVI, 10 (March 14, 1969), 74A; *The Choices,* p. ix; see also "What's the Matter with America," *Harper's Magazine,* CXCIV (March, 1947), 237-39; "The Meaning of Norman Thomas," *America,* CXX (January 4, 1969), 5.

15. Seidler, p. 292.

16. "You Can't Vote Again for Norman Thomas," *The Christian Century,* LXX (January 7, 1953), 4–5.

17. "An American Conscience," *Time,* XCII, 26 (December 27, 1968), 18.

18. Harrington, review of *Norman Thomas: Respectable Rebel* and *Great Dissenters,* p. 66.
19. "Norman Thomas," *The New Yorker,* XLIV, 45 (December 28, 1968), 21.
21. "The Meaning of Norman Thomas," p. 5.
21. *Ibid.;* "Norman Thomas," pp. 20–21.
22. Whitman, p. 2E.
23. *The Choices,* pp. vii–x.
24. Harrington, review of *Norman Thomas: Respectable Rebel* and *Great Dissenters,* pp. 64–65. Despite Michael Harrington's criticism of Murray B. Seidler's characterization of Thomas as "a successful failure," Seidler does indicate his awareness of this aspect of Thomas' significance. Seidler, pp. 294–317.
25. Carl N. Degler, *Out of Our Past: The Forces That Shaped Modern America* (New York, 1959), pp. 259–72; David A. Shannon, *The Socialist Party of America: A History* (Chicago, Ill.; 1967), pp. 249–73.
26. Bernard K. Johnpoll, *Pacifist's Progress: Norman Thomas and the Decline of American Socialism* (Chicago, Ill.; 1970).

Selected Bibliography

PRIMARY SOURCES

Norman Thomas Papers

This collection in the New York Public Library consists of 158 boxes of Thomas' personal and official correspondence, drafts of speeches, writings, and miscellaneous papers. A box list prepared by the library staff in 1968 greatly facilitates the use of this massive collection.

Columbia Oral History Project

The transcripts of the three taped interviews with Norman Thomas are located in the Oral History Office, Butler Library, Columbia University. Though not particularly well organized, the transcripts of the interviews contain a wealth of information about the influences which shaped Thomas' writing.

Maurice Goldbloom interview

This interview was conducted by the author on July 29, 1970 in New York City. Mr. Goldbloom, Thomas' longtime personal friend and associate in the Socialist party, provided an interesting assessment of the significance of Thomas as a reform writer.

Recording

"Norman Thomas Reminisces." New Rochelle, N.Y.: Spoken Arts, Inc., 1959.

Books

After the New Deal, What? New York: Macmillan Co., 1936.

America's Way Out: A Program for Democracy. New York: Macmillan Co., 1931.

Appeal to the Nations. New York: Henry Holt & Co., Inc. 1947.

As I See It. New York: Macmillan Co., 1932.

The Choice Before Us: Mankind at the Crossroads. New York: Macmillan Co., 1934.

The Choices. New York: Ives Washburn, Inc., 1969.

The Conscientious Objector in America. New York: B. W. Huebsch, 1923. Reissued as *Is Conscience a Crime?* New York: Vanguard Press, 1927.

Great Dissenters. New York: W. W. Norton & Company, Inc., 1961.
Human Exploitation in the United States. New York: Frederic A. Stokes Company, 1934.
(with Bertram D. Wolfe) *Keep America Out of War: A Program.* New York: Frederic A. Stokes Company, 1939.
Mr. Chairman, Ladies, and Gentlemen: Reflections on Public Speaking. New York: Hermitage House, 1955.
(with Harry W. Laidler, joint editors) *New Tactics in Social Conflict.* New York: Vanguard Press, 1926.
The Prerequisites for Peace. New York: W. W. Norton & Company, Inc., 1959.
Socialism on the Defensive. New York: Harper & Brothers, 1938.
Socialism Re-examined. New York: W. W. Norton & Company, Inc., 1963.
A Socialist's Faith. New York: W. W. Norton & Company, Inc., 1951.
The Test of Freedom. New York: W. W. Norton & Company, Inc., 1954.
War: No Glory, No Profit, No Need. New York: Frederic A. Stokes Company, 1935.
We Have a Future. Princeton, N.J.: Princeton University Press, 1941.
What Is Our Destiny? Garden City, N.Y.: Doubleday & Company, Inc., 1944.
(with Paul Blanshard) *What's the Matter with New York: A National Problem.* New York: Macmillan Co., 1932.

Pamphlets

Democratic Socialism: A New Appraisal. New York: League for Industrial Democracy, 1953.
World Federation: What Are the Difficulties? New York: The Post War World Council, 1942.

Articles

"Can Our Schools Face Facts?" *Progressive Education,* IX (May, 1932), 338–40.
"Can Pacifism Act Against Injustice?" *The World Tomorrow,* VII (July, 1924), 210–12.
"Civil Rights—But Not Conspiracy," *The New York Times Magazine* (January 7, 1951), pp. 11, 41–42, and 44.
"Collective Security and Socialism." *Socialist Review,* VI, 6 (May-June, 1938), 4–5 and 15.
"Credo of an Old-Fashioned Socialist." *The American Mercury,* LVI (April, 1943), 464–69.
"Dangerous Illusions About the Next War." *Socialist Review,* VI, 10 (March–April, 1939), 1–4 and 12.
"Dark Day for Liberty," *The Christian Century,* LIX (July 29, 1942), 929–31.

"The Dissenter's Role in a Totalitarian Age." *The New York Times Magazine* (November 20, 1949), pp. 13, 76, and 78–79.
"Eugene Victor Debs." *Current History and Forum,* XXV (December, 1926), 373–76.
"The Failure of Organized Socialism in America." *The Progressive,* XXIII, 1 (January, 1959), 29-32.
"The Fate of a Gamblers' Civilization," *Current History and Forum,* XXXVI (May, 1932), 155-60.
"Great Challenge of the Dissenter." *The New York Times Magazine* (November 15, 1959), pp. 24, 54, 56, 59, 62, and 64.
" 'Hire Learning' at Ohio State." *The Nation,* CXXXII (June 17, 1931), 654-56.
"Hoosier Hitlerism." *The Nation,* CXLI (September 18, 1935), 324–26.
"I'm Glad I'm Not Running This Time!" *American Magazine,* CLIV, 4 (October, 1952), 19 and 100-03.
"Is Violence the Way?" *The World Tomorrow,* II (May, 1919), 117–20.
"Labor's Greatness—And Some Weaknesses." *The World Tomorrow,* VIII (January, 1925), 8–10.
"The New Deal: No Program of Security." *The Southern Review,* I (1935), 365–72.
"Norman Thomas Tells of Journalism Career," *Editor and Publisher,* LXXXVI, 3 (January 17, 1953), 55.
"The Old System Is Not Adequate," *The Rotarian,* LXVII, 4 (October, 1945), 28–29.
"Pacifism in America." *Playboy,* XV, 12 (December, 1968), 155 and 278–83.
"The Pacifist's Dilemma." *The Nation,* CXLIV (January 16, 1937), 66–68.
"President Johnson's Great Society." *The Christian Century,* LXXXIII (March 9, 1966), 300-03.
"Proposals for Action at Detroit." *The World Tomorrow,* XVII (April 26, 1934), 206-08.
"Puritan Fathers." *The Atlantic Monthly,* CXLVIII (November, 1931), 650–55.
"Reflections of an Old Campaigner." *The Commonweal,* XLI (December 22, 1944), 246–48.
"Reflections on Russia and Revolution." *The World Tomorrow,* III (September, 1920), 259–62.
"Rethinking Socialism." *The Virginia Quarterly Review,* XXXIV (Winter, 1958), 43–54.
"Should Congress Enact the Employment Nondiscrimination Provisions of the Civil Rights Bill?" *Congressional Digest,* XLIII (March, 1964), 92 and 94.
"Socialism: The Way Out for America." *The World Tomorrow,* XIV (March, 1931), 72–74.
"Socialism Upheld." *The World Tomorrow,* XIII (February, 1930), 70–73.

"The Socialist's Way Out for the Negro." *The Journal of Negro Education,* V (January, 1936), 100-04.
"The Status of Radicalism in America." *The World Tomorrow,* IV (December, 1921), 370–71.
"Totalitarian Liberals." *The Commonweal,* XXXVII (January 22, 1943), 342-44.
"A Visit to Tom Mooney." *The Nation,* CXXVII (October 24, 1928), 423–24.
"What of the Church?" *The New World,* I (February, 1918), 42-46.
"What's Right with America." *Harper's Magazine,* CXCIV (March, 1947), 237–39.
"Why I Am a Socialist." *Independent Woman,* XIII (October, 1934), 311 and 332–33.
"The World As I Want It." *Forum,* XCII (October, 1934), 235.

Book Reviews

The Economics of Defense in the Nuclear Age by Charles J. Hitch and Roland N. McKean, *National Security in the Nuclear Age* by Gordon B. Turner and Richard D. Challener, eds., and *On Thermonuclear War* by Herman Kahn. *Saturday Review,* XLIV (February 4, 1961), 17–19 and 33.
Liberty by Everett Dean Martin. *The Saturday Review of Literature,* VI (June 7, 1930), 1101-04.
The Passing of Normalcy by Charles W. Wood. *The Saturday Review of Literature,* VI (February 1, 1930), 689-90.

Letters to Editors

"A Communication." *The New Republic,* XI (May 26, 1917), 109–11.
"Correspondence." *The Christian Century,* LXII (August 15, 1945), 935.
"Correspondence." *The New Republic,* XI (July 7, 1917), 274-75.
"Correspondence." *The New Republic,* XXXIV (May 9, 1923), 296–97.
"Correspondence." *The World Tomorrow,* XV (August, 1932), 239.
"Letter to the Editor." *The Saturday Review of Literature,* IX (October 29, 1932), 201.
"Letters." *The Nation,* CV (August 23, 1917), 198-99.

SECONDARY SOURCES

BALDWIN, ROGER N. "Norman Thomas: A Memoir." *Saturday Review,* LII (April 12, 1969), 41-42. Concise characterization of the importance of personal integrity and conscience as motivating forces in Thomas' life by a longtime, non-Socialist friend.
FLEISCHMAN, HARRY. *Norman Thomas: A Biography.* New York: W. W. Norton & Company, Inc., 1964. Interesting, sympathetic biog-

raphy; presents a clear picture of the wide range of Thomas' reform activities.

HARRINGTON, MICHAEL. Review of *Norman Thomas: Respectable Rebel* by Murray B. Seidler and *Great Dissenters* by Norman Thomas. *The Reporter,* XXV (November 9, 1961), 64–66. Examination of the significance of Thomas' life by a leading young Socialist. Portrays Thomas as the incarnation of the American Protestant sense of social justice and integrity who had failed to bridge the gap between Socialism and the realities of American politics.

JOHNPOLL, BERNARD K. *Pacifist's Progress: Norman Thomas and the Decline of American Socialism.* Chicago, Ill.: Quadrangle Books, 1970. Detailed critical study which blames much of the failure of Socialism in America on Thomas' leadership. This revealing study of Socialist decline overemphasizes Thomas' capacity to prevent it.

LAIDLER, HARRY W. *History of Socialism.* New York: Thomas W. Crowell Company, 1968. Standard survey of the historical origins and nature of Socialism by one of the leading American Socialist theoreticians.

LENS, SIDNEY. *Radicalism in America.* New York: Thomas W. Crowell Company, 1966. General survey of the nature and significance of American radicalism from colonial origins to modern times. Provides the basis of a comparison between the reform activities of Thomas and previous American radicals.

LEVINSON, EDWARD. "Norman Thomas." *Current History and Forum,* XLV, 1 (October, 1936), 71-75. Detailed discussion of the varieties of Thomas' reform activities during the mid-1930's.

SEIDLER, MURRAY B. *Norman Thomas: Respectable Rebel.* 2nd ed. Syracuse, N.Y.: Syracuse University Press, 1967. Most scholarly, thorough biography of Thomas. Concentrates on his role as a Socialist leader and contains a detailed discussion of the influences which shaped his Democratic Socialism.

SHANNON, DAVID A. *The Socialist Party of America: A History.* Chicago, Ill.: Quadrangle Books, 1967. Basic work on the development and decline of the Socialist party in America. In the last chapter, a particularly lucid discussion of the decline of American Socialism emphasizes conditions beyond the control of the party leadership.

STOLBERG, BENJAMIN. "The Reading of the Candidates." *The Bookman,* LXVIII (October, 1928), 148–49. Early assessment of Thomas' reading habits which illustrates his preoccupation with socioeconomic issues.

WHITMAN, ALDEN. "The Great Reformer, Unsatisfied to the End." *New York Times* (December 22, 1968), p. 2E. Prepared in consultation with Thomas, the obituary presents an interesting assessment of the significance of his reform career.

Index

This index is limited to important items in the text, but also includes a selection of references to significant persons and subjects in the Notes. It does not include items in the Chronology. Norman Thomas' works are listed under his name.